THE
BOLD TRUTH
ABOUT INVESTING

TEN COMMANDMENTS
FOR BUILDING
PERSONAL WEALTH

ADAM BOLD

TEN SPEED PRESS
Berkeley | Toronto

Ten Speed Press
PO Box 7123
Berkeley, California 94707
www.tenspeed.com

Distributed in Australia by Simon and Schuster Australia, in Canada by Ten Speed Press Canada, in New Zealand by Southern Publishers Group, in South Africa by Real Books, and in the United Kingdom and Europe by Publishers Group UK.

Cover and text design by Betsy Stromberg
Typesetting by BookMatters

The chart on page 56 is reprinted with permission of Callan Associates.
Portions of this book were previously published in *The Bold Truth about Mutual Funds* (Rockhill Books, 2005).

Library of Congress Cataloging-in-Publication Data
Bold, Adam.
    The Bold truth about investing : ten commandments of investing for building wealth / Adam Bold.
        p.   cm.
    Includes index.
    Summary: "Helps novice and seasoned investors take back control of their financial investments"—Provided by publisher.
    ISBN 978-1-58008-988-3
        1. Investments. 2. Retirement income—Planning. I. Title.
    HG4521.B578   2009
    332.6—dc22

                                                    2008055105

Printed in the United States of America
on recycled paper (30% PCW)

First printing, 2009
1 2 3 4 5 6 7 8 9 10 — 13 12 11 10 09

THE
BOLD TRUTH
ABOUT INVESTING

CONTENTS

For my wife and daughters,
who have accepted quality of time rather than quantity of time.
As I look at my daughters, I am infinitely proud of not only who
they are today but also who they will become in the future.

INTRODUCTION:
THE TEN COMMANDMENTS
OF INVESTING

I BEGAN MY CAREER in financial services more than seventeen years ago. With three generations of accountants already in my family, I seemed destined to become an accountant. My great-grandfather, the oldest child in his family, found his way to the Midwest in the early 1900s in need of a trade, so he became an accountant and established his business in Kansas City, Kansas. Interestingly, he worked from an office located on the same block where two brothers began a rival firm that later became the tax preparation giant H&R Block. Both of my grandfathers were CPAs, and my dad was a CPA and tax attorney. Yes, I truly seemed destined to become an accountant. But destiny doesn't always become reality.

My accounting career got off to an early start. Beginning at age twelve, I spent summers at my grandfather's accounting practice, learning how to reconcile bank accounts and prepare payroll, income statements, and other vital records. So I learned from an early age the importance of understanding financial statements and financial issues. The work was tedious, but invaluable for my eventual livelihood.

Not only did we prepare taxes for various companies, but we also prepared personal taxes for their owners and officers. I frequently saw that most people who actively traded stocks lost money. It was common to see a successful business owner lose 20 percent or more of his stock portfolio in a year. During this time I gained valuable insight into the reality of stock picking.

I worked for my grandfather for several years after college and trained to be an accountant, because after all, an accounting career was my destiny. But again, destiny isn't always reality.

One day in 1991, my grandfather decided he wasn't enjoying the daily grind as much as he once had. Although he had vowed to never retire, my grandfather decided that this was now the right choice after all and he offered me his business. My grandfather's retirement forced me to choose my direction.

The truth was, I didn't enjoy the accounting business, reading columns of numbers every day. I politely declined the offer. So at age twenty-seven, married and expecting our first child, I went to work for Smith Barney.

I chose this path because the world of investments had always intrigued me. I remembered those successful business owners who lost money in the stock market, but I also knew that money could be made in the markets. Both my father and grandfather were investors; it had been natural, when I was born, for them to gift me with stock, and investments and world events were common topics of discussion at the dinner table.

Because I was exposed to discussions of financial investments and accounting principles from an early age, when I went to work for Smith Barney I believed I knew more about the markets than the average guy. But knowledge of the markets and knowledge of how to be a stockbroker are two different things. I quickly learned that I didn't know anything about being a stockbroker.

During my new-hire training, I received a minimal amount of education on investments; the bulk of my training centered around *selling*. I quickly learned that the ability to "cold call" would be essential to my success as a broker.

I suppose I had a knack for cold calling, because I soon became ranked among the top students in my class of sixty. I spent my days sitting in a cubicle with a headset, calling thousands of people to get a handful of clients. It wasn't easy, but I was doing well, very well, and earning a six-figure income.

Over time, however, Smith Barney changed. After two company acquisitions, Smith Barney went from 2,500 brokers to 14,000 brokers. Up until that point, I could sit with a potential client and discuss financial needs and goals. Now Smith Barney began to tell us *what* to sell. When the Smith Barney XYZ Fund came out, I was expected to sell a certain amount of it. About this time, headhunters began calling, and I knew I needed to work for someone else—a company that hadn't been through these mergers and didn't do business this way. I moved on to Prudential Securities.

At Prudential I gained an important insight. I discovered that I love helping people with their investments. I didn't want to sell people something that wasn't going to help them. I wanted people to understand their investments and why some were better suited for them than others. As time went by, I became better and better at helping people.

In the brokerage industry I was selling load funds, because that was all we were allowed to sell. I didn't make as much money selling mutual funds as I did trading stock, but it dawned on me that over the long run, clients holding mutual funds earned a much better return—if they were decent funds—than did the clients who were buying and selling individual stocks. I was making a lot more money from the stock clients, but the clients in mutual funds were more successful in building their wealth.

I needed to head in a new direction again. All at once, in the middle of the night in 1995, it came to me: I would provide advice on mutual funds for a fee basis instead of selling whatever I could get someone to buy on a transactional basis. I could build a business around selling mutual funds.

As an independent investment adviser, with no ties to any company, I opened The Mutual Fund Store with the purpose of helping others build their wealth. You'd think this would be a commonsense approach. Amazingly, thirteen years after launching The Mutual Fund Store in 1996, in 2009 we remain the only national *fee-based* investment advisory organization operating in the vast segment of the market better known as middle America.

Let me explain. *Commission-based* brokers represent the vast majority of the industry. They often focus on the smaller investors, those with $500,000 or less in their portfolio, and they're paid by the transaction, meaning they're paid up front regardless of whether the investment increases or decreases. A 5-percent commission is common. In contrast, a fee-based adviser is paid to manage the client's portfolio; typically the adviser gets the equivalent of 0.5 to 2 percent each year. The adviser's income rises or falls with the portfolio's performance; he has a financial incentive to increase his client's wealth.

Unfortunately for most investors, fee-based advisers typically focus on the wealthier clients, those with at least $500,000 to invest. The Mutual Fund Store is different. We are unique in bringing fee-based investment management to the average American. That's one reason we expanded so quickly, and it doesn't hurt that the ranks of our target market continue to swell.

I like to think that at least some of our success can also be attributed to the fact that we know how to talk in everyday language to our clients. Finances can be complex, confusing, and, to some people, downright boring. In my more than seventeen years in the financial services sector, one thing has become painfully clear to me: some folks simply don't relish the world of securities and high finance the way I do. Investment terms like *expense ratios, liquidity,* and *net asset values* make their eyes glaze.

I have a little trick to spice up all this financial jargon so that retirement planning and other financial topics aren't as tedious. My communication weapon of choice: analogies. They make a fuzzy, abstract concept seem clear and concrete, reinforcing the power of the original idea.

The other reason for our success happened when good fortune smiled from the airwaves. In 1998, Peter Newman, a CPA in the Kansas City market, invited me to be a guest on his radio show. We had some mutual clients, and he was impressed by our investment statements. I had never been on the radio before, but we hit it off. A month later he called me back. Eventually I was a regular on his show, even hosting while he was on vacation.

Soon I landed my own radio broadcast on the same station. My business grew from $10 million under management in 1997 to $50 million by the end of 1998. The business and my radio show were doing really well, and we were able to grow both. Today *The Mutual Fund Show* is a nationally syndicated program airing coast to coast and still expanding to new markets.

The broadcasts are sheer fun. I talk to interesting people and express my views—on everything from where the economy is headed to the scandals that rocked the mutual fund industry in the early years of the twenty-first century to the credit meltdown and resulting stock-market turbulence of 2008. The combination of offering carefully tailored advice to clients of The Mutual Fund Store and explaining sound investment principles to a mass audience via radio is my calling, my passion.

Over the years, as I have guided clients on their investments through The Mutual Fund Store and studied investor behavior in my conversations with callers to *The Mutual Fund Show*, I have realized that I keep coming back to ten broad principles of investments. These principles can help guide the beginning investor as well as reinforce the best instincts of more savvy market players. There is no clearer, more compelling way of stressing the importance of these foundation principles than by presenting them as my Ten Commandments of Investing:

#1—KNOW YOURSELF   Self-knowledge will determine the success of your financial plan. Consider what stage you are at in your life and decide the goals you want to accomplish.

#2—KNOW WHEN TO INVEST   The time to invest is now. But first you'll need to take a few steps to get your financial house in order—like setting up a rainy-day fund and paying off debt.

#3—KNOW YOUR ADVISER   Before you hire a professional financial adviser to invest your money, ask candidates how they are compensated. Find out what their expertise is, and check their disciplinary and employment history. Then discuss how you will communicate and work together to meet your goals.

#4—HAVE A PLAN   To develop a financial plan, you need to establish your goals, diversify your investments, and keep an eye on volatility; you will also need to revisit the plan as your life circumstances change, and adjust it as appropriate.

#5—BE IN THE BEST FUNDS POSSIBLE   Mutual funds provide professional management and diversification. Our goal is to identify funds whose managers have been able to deliver consistently strong returns over extended periods of time.

#6—AVOID *ANY* HIDDEN COSTS   It's smart to be price conscious. You shouldn't let fees alone drive your investment decisions, but you should pay close attention to mutual fund fees and capital gains distributions.

#7—DON'T BUY WHAT YOU DON'T UNDERSTAND   If your financial investment purchase requires a lengthy contract, chances are you don't fully understand today—nor will you understand later—the financial product you are buying.

#8—BE PROACTIVE ABOUT MANAGING YOUR RETIREMENT INVESTMENTS   Don't wait to plan for retirement. There are no loans, grants, or scholarships for retirement, so don't delay your retirement savings for the sake of other needs for which financial options are available.

#9—STICK TO YOUR PLAN   Make sure your investment accounts maintain your chosen asset allocation and check them on a regular basis. If your circumstances or market conditions change, adjust your investments accordingly. But don't make emotional and rash decisions that may hurt your returns and prevent you from reaching your goals.

#10—LIVE WELL, FOR YOU CANNOT TAKE IT WITH YOU!   I'm not saying you should spend foolishly, but what's the point in saving money if you *never* spend it? None of us knows what will happen to us tomorrow, much less when we retire, so learn to enjoy some of your investments along the way.

In the chapters that follow, I will explain each of the commandments and how to take control of your investments. If you have been listening to my show, the book will consolidate the advice you consistently hear. If you're just picking up this book, the ten commandments will give you a thorough introduction to my investment philosophy.

My mission is to help you take responsibility for your investments and reach financial success. Every day, I am responsible to my wife and my children, my extended family, my staff, and the thousands of clients who rely on me to make good investment decisions for them. I am also responsible to the hundreds of thousands of listeners who aren't clients but still listen to my words to determine what to do with their money. With great responsibility comes even greater reward.

I can't begin to describe the satisfaction I feel when clients say that through our investment advice they're putting their kids through college, retiring and managing to meet their personal needs, or purchasing a retirement home. Destiny seemed to hold an accounting career for me, but it turns out my true destiny was to help others invest wisely. The reality is, I love it.

After 2008—one of the worst years in the history of the stock market—my ten commandments are even more relevant and important to follow. Whether you're someone just getting started with investing or you're a more experienced investor who wants to learn how to pick the best mutual funds, this book holds invaluable knowledge to help you along the way.

Commandment # 1

KNOW YOURSELF

**Every investment plan is unique to its investor.
You can't just copy what someone else is doing.**

TO THY OWN SELF BE TRUE. Wise men have reminded us of that basic principle of life for centuries. It should also be a guiding light in investing. Before you can put together an investment plan, you must know what you are trying to accomplish. You also need to know your personal limitations—your strengths and weaknesses.

The first investment commandment, Know Yourself, is vital because self-knowledge will determine the success of your financial plan. First, consider what stage you are at in your life and determine your goals. Goals can range from buying a home and starting your own business to saving for your retirement.

Then ask yourself *how* you want to reach those goals. Do you simply want to not lose any money? If your answer is yes, you would design a portfolio with more safe investments such as money markets funds. Or is your main objective to generate substantial long-term growth? If your answer is yes, then your investments would be more aggressive and growth oriented. And if you're somewhere in between—you want to generate some growth and some income—you should pick a balance of conservative and growth investments.

Also determine what type of return you want to generate from your portfolio. Do you want your investments to simply keep pace with inflation? Or would you prefer your portfolio to beat the stock market's return? Your answers will help determine whether your portfolio should hold investments that are very conservative or very high growth or somewhere in between.

Finally—and perhaps more important—you need to determine how much risk you are willing to take in the markets, as well as how much volatility is comfortable within the value of your portfolio. Unfortunately, the investment industry often defines "knowing yourself" only in reference to risk tolerance. Investment advisers or financial articles and books will often ask, "Are you a conservative investor, a moderate investor, or an aggressive investor?" But risk tolerance is hard to quantify or describe. In my opinion, those descriptors are too broad and can mean too many different things.

On any given day, people are worried about their investments becoming worth less. Certainly, nobody is happy when their investments go down. However, most people can live with some occasional losses, because they understand that they have to accept some downside in exchange for making money when things go well. Others cannot sleep if they see their account statement and the value is one penny less than they put in. Still others are most troubled when the market goes up 20 percent and their holdings only go up 10 percent. They tell themselves, "Gosh, I should have been more aggressive, so I could have gotten that 20 percent." Or if they lose 20 percent in a market that is down 30 percent they say, "I can't believe that I lost 20 percent of my money."

When you're able to accept that you're going to lose money from time to time, you're more apt to know what your limits are. There are a few questions you can ask yourself to discover how much risk you are willing to take and still sleep soundly at night. For example, if you look at your current portfolio, and your account was worth 10 percent less than the month before, what would you do?

1. Sell everything right away.

2. Be concerned, but just continue to monitor your investments.

3. Put in more money, because this is a great opportunity.

If you chose the first answer, you probably don't like to see volatility, or big swings, in the value of your portfolio. If you chose the second one, you're apt to be calmer and will wait before pulling the trigger. And if you chose the third answer, you can handle swings more easily and are willing to take more risk (and to seize the opportunity to "buy low").

This Q&A challenges you to think about your actions and motivations. It's a much better approach than simply labeling yourself a conservative, moderate, or aggressive investor. Once you determine your goals, how you want to achieve those goals, and your level of comfort with risk and volatility, you can design your portfolio to suit your personality and needs.

Of course, knowing yourself and acting on this knowledge are two different things. Also, you must have realistic expectations about achieving your financial goals. For example, an investor may take pride in being very conservative in her investment approach, but if all of her money is plopped in very safe investments, she may not be able to amass enough money over time to meet her goals. Here are some bad investment behaviors that you should avoid.

Passive Investing

One big obstacle to self-awareness for most people is inertia. It's always easiest to do nothing. Some folks look at the investments they hold and convince themselves that standing still is the safest option. They might think: "I know these investments are not as good as they can be, but to change them would be a hassle."

I don't like to say these people are "lazy." Let's just say they are inattentive. They put their money in Fund A and forget about it. Whether it does poorly or well, they are just not doing much to stay on top of it.

Other people tend to fear the unknown. They are very uncomfortable with the idea of putting their hard-earned money in a market that can move up and down for no good reason at any time—and they can't control how their investments react. Some people might believe investing is akin to gambling: they have a chance to win big, but they can also lose their shirt if they bet wrong.

I have one client, a single parent in her early forties, who is also my cousin. Because of our family connection, I talk to her a little more frankly than I would to my typical client. Each time we saw each other at holidays, she would say, "I really need to come in and have you look at my investments." But inertia kicked in and she never did. Finally, she came into the office at the beginning of 2003 with a relatively small sum of money to invest. At the same time, she opened a folder and pulled out statements for her 401(k) retirement account, which was fully invested in money market funds. I immediately told her she needed to put a good portion of the funds into other investments and sketched out a variety of places that would make sense and provide her with a balanced portfolio.

One year later, we sat down to have a year-end review. I showed her the performance of her account, where we had invested in mutual funds. It had done very well, growing 35 percent. I asked about her 401(k). Despite my recommendations, she had not moved a dime of her funds out of the money market funds. "At least I didn't lose any money," she sheepishly said. I quickly did some calculations. I then informed her that had she invested her 401(k) funds in the variety of mutual funds I had recommended one year earlier, she would have made a profit of $35,000 instead of $3,000. I watched her face, and I could see the cartoon light-bulb go on above her head. She finally realized that her fear of *losing* money was actually *costing* her money, and that could very well mean that she would not have adequate financial resources to retire one day. In other words, she was playing not to lose.

If you find yourself not acting on your investments—if you find that you are a passive investor—you should understand that doing nothing could hurt you financially later in life. Once you're ready to act—and are able to overcome your fears and determine your comfort zones—especially how much volatility in your investments you can handle—you'll be able to make confident investing decisions. Then, when you discover the investments that fit your personality, goals, and risk tolerance, you'll be able to see your investments grow over time, putting you on the road to financial success.

Ignoring Investment Mistakes

No matter how comfortable we are with our decisions, there will be times when we make the wrong ones. That's life. In fact, mistakes often teach us valuable lessons.

The problem is, acknowledging a mistake is hard. When it comes to investing, the key is to be able to admit when you have made a mistake, recognize it relatively quickly, and move on to something else. Too many investors will continue to suffer their mistakes instead of moving on. Here's how it happens: A broker or an adviser recommends an investment to a client, and it goes down in value. The broker will tell his disappointed client, "Just hold on to it. It will come back." Sometimes it will. In many instances, however, the broker is really saying "hold on" to this not because it is a sound investment but because he doesn't want to look stupid to the client by admitting he made a mistake.

Even without the help of a broker or an adviser, some investors tend to have false hope that a bad investment will eventually turn around, so they cling to it for too long. Sometimes you just have to accept a loss from a bad investment and move on. There are three reasons why you would sell:

1. The investment does not meet the criteria you had for it when you purchased it. For example, a mutual fund's manager has changed.

2. There is something better that you should own than what you currently own.

3. You need the money for some other purpose.

At some point you, the wise investor, have to tell yourself—and your advisers—that no matter how good the original idea was, the investment is not working—so let's move on to something else.

Lack of Emotional Self-Control (or Constant Worriers)

Then there are those who are so emotional that they make rash decisions that end up costing money. These are the people who panic and sell everything when the market is down for a few days or months—as we experienced in the early years of the twenty-first century, and again in 2008. Then, when the market goes back up, they jump back in with buckets of cash. Or they never invest again.

One investor in Las Vegas came to our local Mutual Fund Store and told us he had been trading stocks on his own at home. He monitored every blip in the stock market on handsome computer monitors. He would sit and watch CNBC and other market coverage on these monitors, and the intra-day gyrations would compel him to do something. Over a three-year period, out of all his trades, only two were profitable. Finally he came to us. "I need to have you guys manage this money," he said. One month after opening an account with us, the stock market took a hit and went down every day for a week. Without calling us, our Las Vegas friend, on a Friday, sold everything in his account. On Monday, the Dow went up 200 points. He called us again and said, "I made a horrid mistake. I need to get that money back into the market."

This time I had a conversation with him and said we would love to manage his money—but he had to be less impulsive. He agreed. One week later, the market went through another gyration and he once again sold when prices were at their lows. That gentleman knew himself intellectually but emotionally couldn't control himself. Finally, he let go and let us manage his account in the way we thought appropriate. I am not exaggerating when I tell you that he is now one of our happiest clients. Not only because his investment returns improved, but also because the big emotional burden has been lifted from his shoulders.

Through the bear market of 2000 to 2002, we had a lot of clients who did very similar things. The terrible part about that bear market was that it lasted for three years. Everybody assumes that from time to time things will go down on the way to going up. In 2000, the market started going down. Some investors immediately bailed out. Others could make it through one year, but after two years of a bear market they sold everything. After three consecutive bad years, some investors told themselves: "The stock market is never going to go back up again," and they jumped out. When the stock market came roaring back in 2003, a lot of people did not benefit from the upturn because they had bailed out of the market. Essentially, they suffered a double whammy—they lost money when the market was down, and they lost opportunity when the market went up. Many individual investors wait until they have full confidence in the market, and by that time much of the recovery has already taken place.

Unfortunately, too many people didn't learn this lesson. As the economic crisis plays itself out in 2008 and 2009, people spooked by market volatility have been pulling out their investments or moving them to cash or bonds. For some, this move will severely undermine their long-term financial goals.

I have a strategy to prepare myself for times when the market is particularly volatile and I feel jittery. It's simple: When days are slow and the market calm, I sit and write notes, posing a variety of "what ifs." What would I do if the Dow Jones Industrial Average dropped 600 points in a day? Or soared 600? The answer usually depends on the circumstances in the market, and whether there are short-term or long-term issues affecting the movements.

For example, I try to figure out whether there's a fundamental change in the economic environment that could eventually hurt many companies' earnings. An example of an event with long-term ramifications is the September 11, 2001 terrorist attacks, which had lasting effects on the country, economic activity, and the markets. The housing meltdown and credit crisis caused the stock market and economic growth to drop sharply in 2008, but the long-lasting effects are still unknown. A short-term issue could be something that causes one major company to report bad earnings.

I try to envision a range of scenarios, then compose my responses. So when the market does take a big drop, as it did in 2008, I look at the notes to myself. It's the rational Adam talking to the emotional Adam. Let's think! I've gone through the paces already. Most events should not change my reasons for owning a mutual fund or other investment—and my asset allocation should reflect my goals and time horizons no matter what happens. When I start tinkering with my financial plan, my emotional side is taking over instead of my rational side.

Despite the volume of sound advice out there about sticking to an investing plan even in crises as scary as the one that began in 2008, you'd be surprised how many investors are reactionary. They hear the market is down 300 points, and all the talking heads on TV are yakking about it and scaring the pants off everybody. It's OK to feel scared by the market when things pull back. It's OK to feel bad about the market and to be disappointed. However, it is not OK to make investment decisions emotionally. You should never make financial decisions that way. You need to make them intellectually. If you are one of those people who cannot separate your emotions from your actions, you probably should hire a trustworthy, knowledgeable financial adviser to make your investment decisions.

Investor Success Syndrome

Some investors are too cautious; others do not exercise sufficient self-restraint. I deal with many entrepreneurs who are natural risk takers. They are comfortable with the volatility of the market and, indeed, thrive on it. Some get to a point where they've been successful over the years and have accumulated large amounts of money. They will come to me and say they want to be very aggressive and "swing for the fences."

It's difficult to get such people to reassess their attitudes. Here's what I try to tell them: "Right now, you're earning $X per year. Now with this money that you've accumulated, if we get a 3 percent rate of return we can generate the same amount of income with you not working as you make when you're working. There's no reason to take a 'swing-for-the-fences' risk when you don't need to. You don't need a 40-percent return to maintain your lifestyle."

Once these risk takers see the danger they're putting their portfolio in, they usually agree to scale back on the investments that carry the most risk. The trick with this group is to find a balance of reasonable risk that will also provide a rate of return that they're happy with.

Fear of Not Investing

Here's another personality type: I meet a lot of people of retirement age who have saved money all through their life and have accumulated considerable wealth. When they prepare to retire, they find it very difficult to spend their money and to reduce their investments. They feel a need to make sure their money keeps accumulating. I tell those people, "Look, the reason that you accumulated this money was so that you could ultimately spend it—now."

If your portfolio is generating more money than you spend, then ultimately all you're going to do is leave a bigger estate for your kids. One of my philosophies is that whether you leave $50,000, $500,000, or $5 million to your children, they should be appreciative. That's money that *you* worked for, not money that *they* worked for.

If you can enjoy your life more, you should do that. People who can afford to should take more vacations and do what they enjoy most—that's why they worked hard to accumulate a nest egg. When people retire, they have to change their mind-set. It is not easy. But once they're comfortable with spending their hard-earned money and investments, they can really enjoy life.

Knowing Your Best Self

Knowing yourself is one thing. Knowing your *best* self is quite another. After reading this chapter, you may decide that you want to change your "investment" self or change those investment behaviors that have prevented you from building wealth. The way to do so is by educating yourself. Managing your own investments is a lot of work, but you can do it. If you're too busy, then you should hire a professional adviser to help you (we discuss how to do this in chapter 3). By reading this book you are one step closer to knowing your *best* self. The more you learn, the more able you'll be to discern what investments are appropriate for you and what is not and to draft the best possible investment plan that works for *you*.

KNOW WHEN
TO INVEST

**Before you start saving money for the future,
consider what may be costing you money right now.**

NOW THAT YOU HAVE DETERMINED your investment goals and how to meet those goals, it's time to evaluate when to start investing.

So when should you invest? Getting started with investing is not hard, but it does take some time and effort, and you must make important decisions about what works for you. First, you'll need to take a few steps to get your financial house in order:

1. Get rid of any bad debt. There is good debt, bad debt, and reasonable debt; I'll explain the differences.

2. Build up a so-called rainy-day fund. This is the pool you'll need to tap if your furnace springs a leak, the car breaks down, or the kids need braces. Your rainy-day money should be accumulated *before* you start to invest and save for your retirement, children's education, or any other major financial goal.

Once you have taken care of those first two fundamentals, you're cleared for investing.

Paying Off Debt

For most would-be investors, getting into a regular habit of saving first requires managing personal debt acquired over the years and eliminating the *bad* debt. Let's separate the bad from the good.

Mortgage interest is good debt. When I die, I just might have a mortgage. I will likely never fully pay it off, because mortgage debt is good debt. Many people—mistakenly, I believe—are in a big hurry to pay off their homes. People have an innate belief that if you "own the farm," the bank can't take it away. But we don't live in the Depression era; even in our tough economic times, we live in a very different world today than we did eighty years ago.

I bought a new house in 2003 and was able to get a 5.5-percent mortgage, and the interest I pay on it is tax deductible. So in my tax bracket I save, right off the top, roughly one-third of my interest payments in the form of lower taxes. One-third of 5.5 percent is roughly 1.8 percent. So my net cost of funds is about 3.7 percent. Now the question is, can I take the money that I would otherwise use to pay down my mortgage and earn more than 3.8 percent a year on it? Every dollar that I earn over 3.7 percent is an incremental dollar that I will someday have available to me for retirement or for other uses. Thus, mortgage debt is good debt; it makes sense to carry that debt.

This doesn't mean that people who have lived in their house for thirty years and have paid off their mortgage should go out and get a new mortgage and invest the money in the stock market. In some cases that may be appropriate, but in most it is not. However, I don't think that the person who is still paying off a home should be in any big hurry to pay the debt down.

Other common types of personal debt are student loans and car loans. These loans also don't have to be paid off completely before you start to invest. A student loan can provide a return on a big investment in *yourself*, as long as you don't overpay for a degree and can eventually find a good job and salary. I think it's better to spend $40,000 on a four-year state college rather than $200,000 for an Ivy League school— especially if you decide to get an art history degree and stand to earn $25,000 after graduation.

I consider car loans to be an essential cost that is included in lifestyle and living expenses. After all, very few people are lucky enough to be able to walk to work these days. I can understand why people finance cars, and I don't really have a problem with that—if they choose a car with payments within their means. A banker friend, however, recently described a client who earns $3,000 a month who bought a new Chevy Suburban and faces car payments of $700 a month. That is way too much debt for that gentleman to shoulder. Consider keeping a car that you've paid off instead of buying a new car that would require another loan. That way, you can put more money in your investment portfolio.

Credit card debt not paid off in full each month is bad debt. Basically, if you can't afford to pay for something, you should not buy it. Just because you can buy something doesn't mean you should. When you're at Home Depot to get lightbulbs and you spot that shiny gas grill with a sign offering "0% Financing!"—take a moment and ask yourself whether you're going to be upset if you don't have that grill when you get home. If the answer is no, walk away. Credit cards should be used only for emergency situations, such as your furnace breaking or a necessary car repair, after you've used your rainy-day money.

One of our clients is a cocktail waitress at a casino. She earns $45,000 a year, half in salary, half in tips. When she came to us, she owed $19,000 to twelve different credit card companies charging interest of 18 to 21 percent. That's a budget breaker right there. She has always paid on time and has good credit—just too much of it. I called the credit card company she owed the most to and said, "I've got in my hand a low-rate introductory offer from a rival credit card company good for six months. I am advising my client to move her balance over—unless there is anything you can do to help." They immediately reduced her interest rate from 21 percent down to 12 percent just because we asked. Consider the impact of saving 9 percent on $3,000!

Next, I asked my client whether at the end of the month, after paying her bills, she could come up with $50 or $100. Previously, each month she would use leftover funds to go to a baseball game or dinner out, so the money disappeared. I said, "Here is what I want you to do. We have this list of credit card balances. Each month, I want you to send an extra $100 to the account with the smallest balance. Make your regular payment, plus the extra $100. After four months, one card will be paid off. After that balance is gone, send the next company your regular payment, plus the amount you were paying on the one that is now paid off, plus the extra $100. Keep taking out the small balances first."

The reason for this approach is twofold. First, of course, it reduces costly interest payments. But second, it provides the client with a real sense of accomplishment. I wanted her to have that. Over a period of two years she could probably get all that debt knocked down. Now, every time I see her she excitedly tells me which cards have been paid off. She took her tax refund and plowed half into paying off credit card debt. By paying off those balances at 18 to 21 percent, she's earning an 18 to 21 percent rate of return on that money. That is a handsome return!

As we have seen, debt in itself is not wholly evil—as long as it does not balloon to excessive proportions. Too often, people buy things because they want them, not because they need them. If you look around your house, how much stuff do you have that you wanted but could have lived without? Curbing your consumer appetites, paying as you go for what you buy, and avoiding mountainous credit card debt all go hand in hand with executing an effective approach to building up your savings to achieve your investment strategy.

Rainy-Day Money

With the bad debt paid off, you can turn to building up your rainy-day money. Again, you should fund this financial safety net *before* you start to invest savings for your retirement, children's education, or any other major financial goal.

Some folks put this rainy-day money in a simple checking or savings account. Although money in such accounts is readily accessible, it usually won't earn any interest. I suggest you make your money work a bit harder—stash it in the highest-yielding money market account you can find. That way your money may at least stay ahead of inflation. Money market accounts are designed to be a safe place to store money that you might need access to quickly. You certainly don't want to risk losing your rainy-day money by investing it in a mutual fund or individual stocks.

People traditionally have been told to keep three to six months' worth of expenses on hand in cash or money market accounts in case they lose their jobs or face some other emergency. In other words, if they routinely spend $4,000 a month on mortgage, food, and other necessities, they should have $12,000 to $24,000 they could get to easily—without cashing in bonds and mutual funds or cracking open a 401(k), all of which will trigger tax or penalty consequences.

Years ago, when I started in this industry, I agreed with that three-to-six-months philosophy. But now I'm modifying my tune. Two months' worth of expenses—three, tops—is plenty to suffice in most emergencies that people have to deal with. Why the change? To me it's worth the gamble to invest a bit more toward long-term goals, such as your retirement, and a bit less toward just-in-case scenarios. If you store away too much money in a liquid account such as a checking or saving account, you could miss out on generating higher returns from your investments.

Let's say Tom puts away $100 a month, and it takes two years to accumulate two months' worth of living expenses for his rainy-day money. Then Tom can invest that $100 a month in a growth mutual fund. If Tom loses his job after three years, he will have access to his rainy-day money, plus he can tap a year's worth of growth from the mutual fund. But he should sell some of his mutual fund holdings only if they have grown in value. If the mutual fund is down in value, he shouldn't sell it—he should use his rainy-day money instead. Then, if he runs out of rainy-day money, he can access his available lines of credit. The money from his rainy-day pool and credit lines should hold him over until he finds another job.

Even in the toughest of economic times, like those that began in 2008, it's important to set aside the rainy-day money and *then* invest in mutual funds, so that you always have a cushion if something terrible happens. Once your rainy-day fund is established, then you should begin fully funding your retirement accounts. If you have children, and have money to spare, then you can start a fund to pay for their education. But remember, you have to invest and save for your own retirement before socking away money in your kids' college fund. There are many ways to pay for college, including scholarships, grants, and loans, but there are no scholarships or free rides to pay for your retirement.

Also keep in mind that you're building up your rainy-day fund so that you have money in case you have an emergency home or car repair, have unreimbursed medical expenses, or lose your job. You should not tap your rainy-day money to pay for a big-ticket item such as a home or car—you should save enough money for the down payment in your savings or money market account. You also shouldn't try to invest in mutual funds or stocks to raise money to buy a car or home, because with market ups and downs it could take too long, and timing the purchase for a market upswing could prove difficult.

Develop the Discipline to Save and Invest

With bad debt paid off and some rainy-day dollars stashed away, you are ready to start investing.

The key to building wealth is developing the discipline of both saving and investing. Young people just starting their careers often will say, "I'm going to wait until I get $10,000 and then I am going to invest it." I contend that if you wait until you get a large sum of money together you'll never get there, because if the money is in your checking account you will likely spend it.

Actually, the longer you wait to start saving and investing, the more you'll have to save and the longer you'll have to do it. If you start investing in your twenties, you'll have more money to buy things in your thirties and forties because you started investing earlier. If you're a disciplined saver and investor, you'll be able to retire younger—perhaps at age sixty-five, rather than seventy-five or eighty if you start later in life.

To start investing, you can establish an automatic investment plan so that every month, on the same date, $50 will be transferred from your checking account to your account at a mutual fund. If you have $50 or $100 to spare in your checking account, you will spend it. Count on it. You'll go out to dinner or you will buy clothes or shoes you've been wanting. If that money has already been taken out of your account, your lifestyle will probably not be affected.

If you can save and invest $100 a month, then after a year you'll have $1,200 in the mutual fund account—and perhaps even more, assuming your investment grows in value. After two years you'll have at least $2,400. As time goes by, you won't even notice the $100 a month coming out of your checking account; you will just get used to it. When you get a raise, increase your monthly contribution from $100 to $200 a month. Over a period of time, just raise the amounts that you are putting in. Your investments will build up quickly. Eventually you will look at your account and be surprised to see you have $5,000.

It's never too late to start. Often, workers who are in their thirties and forties and in the middle of their careers and haven't started to invest (or invest very little) delay it further by saying, "Well, it will take me so long to catch up, what's the difference?" Here's the difference: if you don't start now, you should be prepared to work much longer and later in life.

Sometimes all you need is a little motivation. Think about the casual jogger who decides to run a marathon. The jogger will have to make time to strengthen his body for the physical strain and work up the stamina to run this long distance. Each week of training, the jogger gets stronger and is able to run a few more miles than he could before. Pretty soon, the jogger is up to eighteen or twenty miles, and eventually he will work up to the marathon distance. If I were that jogger, I'd be pretty proud of this accomplishment. Like the jogger, who at the start of his training must have seen the length of the marathon as a daunting prospect, you may feel intimated when you are told you need to save 12 percent of your salary yearly for retirement. You may never be able to do that, but you have to start somewhere. Once you feel like you've accumulated some personal net worth, you'll want to keep going and complete that long-term financial goal—your financial marathon.

Another piece of advice: don't look back. Look at the Kansas City Royals baseball team, which has struggled at the bottom of their division for four or five years in a row. Or take the Chicago Cubs, who haven't won a World Series trophy in one hundred years. Does that mean these teams shouldn't try to win? No. They want to win, and I will keep going to Royals baseball games in the hope that someday they will. So if you haven't saved to invest yet or your investments have not paid well recently, don't lose faith: get started, and keep going. You can't change the past, but you can make the future better. Have faith that you can become a good investor.

KNOW YOUR ADVISER

Just because your potential advisers are nice people doesn't mean that they should be your adviser. You need to know how they get paid. What motivates them? Do they have any hidden agendas?

ONCE YOU HAVE DETERMINED whether you are in a position to start investing right away or can make plans to start investing in the next few months, the next step—turning to experts to help you achieve your objectives—may seem easy. However, it is not. Who you turn to has huge implications for the outcome of your investment planning. Take great care in picking your advisers, because your choice will potentially pay vast dividends.

Maybe you have decided that you are not the best person to develop and implement a multifaceted investment strategy to best nurture your personal investments. There is no shame there. It is no admission of personal weakness or failure. It does not reflect on the soundness of your education. You are not flawed. Your children and dog will not hate you. Perhaps you recognize that you could educate yourself to be a smart investor, but prefer not to because you would rather spend time with your family, work at your career—or go fishing. Other priorities reign in your life.

You also are convinced that investments are too important to be locked in a drawer and forgotten. You recognize that an investment strategy must be developed and then executed over time. You therefore set out to recruit someone in the best position to provide sound, rewarding investment advice on an ongoing basis.

There are armies of candidates eager for the assignment. Yet it is surprising that many of us do not give much thought to how to evaluate the hordes of financial planners, stockbrokers, and others eager to tell us where *they* would like to put *your* money, if only given the chance.

Here's a quick test. Jot down all the investment retirement accounts you have opened with employers you have worked for over the years, all the mutual fund accounts you have set up, all the brokerage accounts you hold. Have you ever met, face-to-face, the investment advisers listed on your quarterly statement? There is a good chance that you haven't. If you once did, odds are that that person is no longer working for the firm, and the person whose name is listed as your representative "inherited" your account.

You would never turn the proceeds of your paycheck over to someone you do not know. Yet chances are that you, like most everyone, are willing to leave the funds you set aside for your future well-being, your children's education, and your twilight years in the hands of a total stranger.

If you take nothing else from the book you now hold in your hands, be resolved that you will never again blissfully entrust your personal riches to anyone you do not know. Your financial adviser should be someone you know—or a very close friend knows—and can trust. That's why my third commandment that will help you achieve financial success is "Know Your Adviser."

Before you hand over your hard-earned money to a financial adviser, you need to sit face-to-face and interview him or her. And when you do, ask one of the most important questions: "How are you compensated?" Simply put, is this person providing advice to you or selling products— thus benefiting a third party, but perhaps not you?

What Type of Adviser Is Right for You?

Everyone, it seems—every friend, neighbor, and uncle—has advice about financial planning, or they know someone who's good at it. Beyond that, there are more than 5,000 brokerage firms and 665,000 registered securities representatives in this country, and I'd wager half of them are ready to slip you their business card.

According to the Securities and Exchange Commission (SEC), as a general rule, every adviser and firm that gets paid to give investing advice must register with either the SEC or the state securities agency where they're headquartered. To check whether an adviser is properly registered, read her registration forms—the two-part Form ADV. The first part of the Form ADV provides information about the adviser's business and whether she's had problems with regulators or clients. The second part explains the adviser's services, fees, and strategies. The SEC recommends that before you hire an adviser, you should always ask for and carefully read both parts of the Form ADV. You can check an adviser's most recent Form ADV by visiting the Investment Adviser Public Disclosure (IAPD) website, www.adviserinfo.sec.gov.

So how exactly do you go about finding the right person to help you with your investments? First, you should learn about and understand the different types of advisers and brokers, as well as how they are compensated.

Brokers

Commission brokers represent the vast majority of the industry. They're paid by the transaction, meaning they're paid up front, regardless of whether the stock, bond, mutual fund, or other investment rises or falls over time. A 5-percent commission is common. Spend $10,000 buying a load mutual fund from a commissioned broker, and about $500 goes to the broker as a commission. That's his payment.

As you can imagine, I have reservations about the commission-based approach. I believe in my heart that most of these advisers are good people, and they want their clients to do well and live prosperous lives. But because they get paid based on the transaction—not on how well the investment performs over time—there's no financial impact on the commission broker if the investment climbs or crumbles. He's pocketed his commission regardless.

There's another reason for my concern. When you pay that commission, you start in a hole. Put $10,000 into a load fund—that is, a mutual fund that generates a commission charge—and the broker takes out his $500 commission. You now have $9,500 in your account. The account must grow $500 *just to get even.*

You might think that's OK, because you're paying for advice. But because you're paying it all up front, you're missing out on the compounding of that $500 over time. Compounding is vital to your investments. Essentially, it means you're making earnings from your earnings, year after year.

Let's say that fund rises 10 percent the first year, boosting your account by $950. It's now at $10,450. That same investment in a no-load fund would be worth $11,000—a $550 difference. (For the sake of illustration, this example doesn't include additional fees or taxes; more on that in chapter 6.) Through the years, there's a geometric progression in which the loss of that $500 load becomes ever more pronounced. The good news is that there are many, many no-load mutual funds. It's foolish to pay a load for a fund.

There's yet another reason I don't like loads. The National Association of Securities Dealers (now known as the Financial Industry Regulatory Authority, or FINRA) prohibits commissioned brokers from "churning"—moving clients from one mutual fund to another just to generate another commission. So if you buy a load fund, you can switch funds within that fund family without commission. But if you want to switch funds outside that family, you pay a commission. Because the regulatory authorities are very sensitive to churn, brokers don't switch their clients often. You end up tethered to one fund family. Needless to say, no single fund family has a lock on all the good mutual funds. That's why, when we recommend funds, it's "one from this family, one from that family." You should also keep in mind that a broker's investment advice is usually based on that firm's research. During my stint at Smith Barney in Kansas City, the firm had research analysts who provided coverage on about 400 stocks. Of those 400 stocks, about 397 were either buy- or hold-rated. There were only three stocks rated as a "sell"! When I was a broker at Smith Barney, I had to pick from those "highly rated" 250 stocks and figure out which ones to sell to my clients. What they taught me in training was to sell the securities that had the best stories. When I called a client to get him to do a transaction, I had to come up with a convincing story. I remember recommending the stock of a biotechnology company founded by Jonas Salk, the developer of the polio vaccine. With Salk, I had a great story to tell. I didn't need to get bogged down with my client in a detailed discussion about the financial fundamentals of the company.

Also common during my days at Smith Barney was the "squawk box"—little speakers on our desks. All of a sudden, they would come to life and a remote voice would intone, "We have ten thousand shares of Stock X in our inventory, and if you sell shares to our clients we will pay you an extra fifty-cents-per-share commission." The client, of course, was clueless about all this. I would wonder, if Smith Barney didn't want Stock X in its inventory, why would my clients want it in theirs?

On top of needing to evaluate the merits of the recommended investment, you are forced to wonder, every time a broker makes a recommendation, whether he is recommending a product because it's good for you or because he needs to boost his income. When I worked for Smith Barney, if I could get you to buy something, I'd get paid. If I could get you to sell it, I'd get paid again. If I could get you to buy something else with the proceeds, I'd get paid again. If you made a wise investment and kept if for the next ten years, I never got paid again. Talk about a situation ripe for conflict of interest!

This problem also applies to mutual funds. The broker sells you a load fund and gets his commission up front. So this week he gets a paycheck. But next week, if he wants a paycheck, he has to find somebody else to ring up a sale and register a commission. Because there are only so many hours in a week, over time he'll be too busy searching for new clients and not much interested in following up with you. Clearly he's a salesperson, not an adviser.

In fact, there are a variety of ways that mutual fund companies and brokerage houses motivate their staff to sell certain products, which could end up keeping fees high and hurting investors' returns. Especially common—and unscrupulous—is something called "shelf space" fees. Many brokerages have a "preferred list" of mutual funds. To gain a spot for their fund on this coveted listing, a mutual fund firm may send bundles of money to the brokerage. Disclosed in fine print, these fees represent the industry's most galling ethical breach.

Edward Jones, for example, had a preferred fund list that it would tout to clients. As a client, you probably would think that a fund gets onto the list because of superior performance. However, the reality is that a fund would get on that list when the fund company paid Edward Jones perhaps $500,000 to $1 million, plus 30 percent of their ongoing management expenses. In 2002, 85 percent of Edward Jones's sales were funds on the preferred list. A remarkable coincidence? I think not. Jones paid a $75 million fine for the lack of disclosure to its clients.

You should also steer clear of a broker or an adviser who works for a mutual fund company and pushes that company's products. Those who work for Waddell & Reed, for example, primarily sell Waddell & Reed funds. Any time you're approached by such representatives, ask yourself: "Are they recommending this to me because it's good for me, or are they recommending this because it's good for their company?" Is a Fidelity rep ever going to say, "This is a bad fund" about a Fidelity fund?

If you have your money at a bank and are asked if you need investment help, you should think twice. Banks have expanded from deposits to investment advisory services to make more money. The advisers that work at banks may not be highly qualified to offer the best advice and financial planning. And most of the financial advisers at banks sell only funds that the bank owns or has a stake in. In all likelihood, they are not searching the entire universe of investments to find the very best ones for you. A person with at least $50,000 to invest should have a portfolio containing seven to a dozen different mutual funds (we'll talk more about this in chapter 5). What are the odds that the ten best mutual funds in the world are from one family of mutual funds? Pretty slim.

Commissions and fees represent the basics of how brokers and financial advisers get paid. But there are other, more hush-hush forms of compensation. For instance, mutual fund firms often underwrite an adviser's client-appreciation event or a three-day "marketing seminar" (read: paid vacation) to vacation spots like Hawaii.

Many of the fee and commission practices have been around Wall Street for a long time—but some of the unethical methods have been curbed. A few years ago, major scandals broke out on Wall Street after it was disclosed that respected brokerages such as Merrill Lynch were publishing research reports saying that a stock was a "buy" although privately the analyst would tell coworkers that the stock was junk and should be sold.

As investors learn about the various practices just described, they realize they need to ask more questions. And again, the primary question to ask a potential broker is how he or she wishes to be compensated. So the next time a broker says, "This is what you want," counter with a few choice questions: "How are you paid? And in what *other ways* is your firm compensated?" Then ask yourself whether he's selling these funds because it's best for you—or because it's best for his company.

These brokers are not evil. They aren't trying to do the wrong thing, but the system is set up in such a way that in order for them to be successful they have to think about themselves first, rather than you the client.

Fee-Based Financial Advisers

Unlike a broker who gets paid on commission, a fee-based financial adviser takes a portion of the portfolio he manages for a client, typically the equivalent of 0.5 to 2 percent each year. That way the adviser's income rises or falls with the portfolio's performance, and he has a financial incentive to increase his client's wealth.

For instance, a fee-based adviser who manages $500,000 for a client will receive about $5,000 a year. If that portfolio grows to $600,000 the next year, the adviser receives $6,000. Unfortunately for most investors, fee-based advisers typically focus on the wealthier clients—those with at least $500,000 to invest. That's what's unique about us at The Mutual Fund Store—we brought fee-based investment management to the average American.

Advisers are supposed to determine investors' time horizons, their risk tolerances, and their goals and aspirations. Because there's no such thing as a standard investment adviser, you need to know about their qualifications. Equally important is the adviser's area of expertise. Here are some of the most common titles you'll come across in your search.

Certified Financial Planner (CFP): A certified financial planner is a common type of adviser. The CFP is kind of an all-encompassing title: it means the person is capable in a host of financial areas, such as estate planning, taxes, and insurance. To earn a CFP designation, an adviser must take an educational CFP Board-Registered Program and pass a ten-hour certification exam and must also have at least three years' full-time experience as a financial planner.

After that, the CFP has to sign the CFP board's code of ethics, which puts clients' interests first, and comply with the Financial Planning Practice Standards, which outlines what clients should be able to reasonably expect from the adviser.

Chartered Mutual Fund Counselor (CMFC): A Chartered Mutual Fund Counselor is an adviser who, in addition to her Registered Investment Adviser (RIA) certification, has received additional education in the area of mutual funds and has ongoing education requirements. CMFCs must meet ethical requirements and have signed an ethics pledge before they get in the door, as well as possess a clean disciplinary history. The title represents a collaboration between the College for Financial Planning and the Investment Company Institute (ICI), the primary trade association for the mutual fund industry.

Certified Fund Specialist (CFS): A Certified Fund Specialist is an adviser who can construct a person's portfolio using modern portfolio theory to evaluate financial measurements and benchmarks. This certification is issued by the Institute of Business & Finance (IBF). (I currently sit on the board of advisors at IBF.)

At The Mutual Fund Store, our advisers are all certified as CMFCs, CFSs, or both; these are the premier industry-recognized mutual fund designations.

Certified Public Accountant (CPA): If you need advice about income taxes and tax-efficient investments, make sure your adviser has this designation. To earn a CPA title, a person must pass the Uniform Certified Public Accountant Examination and meet additional education and experience requirements that vary by state.

Chartered Financial Analyst (CFA): This designates an adviser who specializes in stocks, bonds, and other securities. Earning this title, awarded by the CFA Institute of USA, involves undertaking a three-year program that requires candidates to study for and pass three levels of exams. To become a CFA charterholder, candidates must pass all three exams, agree to comply with the code of ethics, pay member dues, and have four years of work experience deemed acceptable by the CFA Institute. CFAs also have to adhere to ethical standards.

Chartered Financial Consultant (ChFC) and Chartered Life Underwriter (CLU): Both of these designations are primarily for insurance agents and are awarded by the American College of Bryn Mawr. To get the ChFC title, an adviser must pass exams covering finance and investing—including income tax, insurance, investment, and estate planning—and have at least three years of experience in the financial industry. A CLU title can be achieved after an adviser completes advanced courses and exams covering insurance, investments, taxes, employee benefits, estate planning, accounting, management, and economics.

You may come across other financial advisers with different titles. Before engaging their services, always confirm their credentials and understand what their area of expertise truly is. Also, beware of anyone titled a *certified senior adviser.* That's one to be leery of. Sure, it sounds like someone who's an expert at advising seniors and retirees. But do a little research on the Web, and you'll discover the truth: just about anyone can pick up the title by paying a fee and taking a few correspondence courses or attending seminars. In a column for the *Kansas City Star*, a respected colleague of mine, Diane Nygaard—who specializes in insurance and securities litigation—warned readers about these self-styled certified senior advisers, as well as *senior tax advisers* (STAs) and *certified long-term care consultants* (CLTCs).

"They build trust by association and through these impressive-sounding, yet meaningless designations," she wrote. "Then they move in for the kill, typically the sale of an annuity."

Nygaard told of an eighty-two-year-old woman who was lured to a free dinner workshop sponsored by the local insurance agent. The woman was persuaded by a "nice young man" bearing a CLTC title to let his staff prepare her taxes. With a road map to her money, he eventually convinced her to convert her investments to a special annuity—which would net him 10 percent of her life savings.

He boasted that the annuity would pay her a 10-percent bonus. What he conveniently neglected to tell her is that she'd need to keep the money in the annuity until she was ninety-six, and there was a 12-percent surrender penalty to get it before then.

Such "financial scam artists," Nygaard observed, "are stirring up an alphabet soup of credentials that is confusing, misleading, and wreaking havoc" on senior citizens' retirement futures.

How to Choose an Adviser

When my wife, who's a surgical nurse by profession and worked in many an operating room, was preparing to give birth to our first daughter, she confided that when it was time for her epidural, there were two anesthetists she didn't want anywhere near her. All the anesthetists at the hospital had similar education and the same medical certifications. But she had witnessed these two sticking needles in other women's backs, and she didn't trust them. Actually, when the time came for the epidural, I'm convinced she would have let *me* put the needle in, but the point is clear: regardless of their certification and training, some people—doctors or financial advisers—are just better at it than others.

The way most people pick their financial adviser is just about the worst method to use: by default. They realize they want help, or they're not happy with their current adviser and want to switch. For a while they don't do anything. They think the worst that can happen is that their returns will flounder a bit while they figure out their next move.

That's not the worst that can happen.

Here's worst: They recognize they have a need, and that makes them easy prey for the first person who approaches them. That person could be a vulture. Picture a customer strolling into a bank and noticing the investment adviser sitting in his tidy cubicle. The customer thinks, "Yeah, I probably should talk to an adviser." The next thing you know, they invest in annuities or proprietary mutual funds sold by the bank.

"But he was so nice," the bank customer tells me later.

Well, of course he was *nice*. But choosing an adviser simply because he or she is polite is a common misstep. The client believes if a financial planner is a neighbor or nephew, belongs to her Rotary Club, or goes to her church, then that qualifies the planner as a wise and gifted investment adviser. It doesn't work that way.

In fact, I'd suggest the financial planner you choose doesn't even have to be in your town. That face-to-face interaction may seem vital to earning your trust, but it doesn't have to be. Our business is driven by data on paper and computer screens. There's little we can't handle through email, fax, and phone. For instance, we typically meet with customers once when they come to an office to meet with an investment adviser, and a second time to review their investment plan after they decide to be clients. After that we rarely see them in person. We make a lot of outbound calls and talk with them several times a year.

So how do you decide which adviser is best for you? It's not like advisers can point to performance results, as if their collective work can be standardized and tracked alongside some financial adviser index. After all, they tailor each portfolio, so each of their clients will see a different return (though clients of similar risk tolerance likely will have similar returns). Still, there are several ways to select an adviser.

Consider how they get compensated. The first thing you should ask, as I explained earlier, is whether the adviser gets paid by commission-only or fee-only. When a broker says, "I am compensated every time I sell something to you," you need to say, "Well, thank you very much, but I need to find somebody else."

In contrast, given that fee-only advisers earn a percentage of your account value over time, generally these advisers will want your portfolio to rise in value. Their pay rises and falls along with your portfolio, giving them incentive to spend the time to make sure you're in the right investments. We'll talk more about hidden costs and fees in chapter 6.

Find out what their expertise is. It's important to consider what areas the adviser specializes in, because those investments may not meet your needs. It's just like choosing a doctor: if you've suffered a heart attack, you want to find a cardiologist, not any other specialist.

Some of our industry's largest brokerage houses, such as JP Morgan and Goldman Sachs, employ thousands of advisers. They're backed by stock analysts, bond analysts, and bankers for IPO deals. The recommendations you get from them depend solely on which guy you meet in which office. Some like stocks, some prefer mutual funds, and others lean toward annuities.

That's why you want to make sure the person you hire as your investment adviser is an expert at what *you* need. Our people are experts at mutual funds and investment management, all using the same investment strategy I personally developed. But we don't sell insurance. If you want advice about insurance and estate planning, we'll refer you to those professionals in the various cities where we operate. If you need tax planning, I will refer you to an accountant. If somebody is looking for a broker or an adviser to help him trade stocks, I don't think I would be the right guy. Although I might be able to make more money selling those other services, it would dilute my ability to be the very best at the things that I do.

Those who have earned a certified financial planner (CFP) designation are trained to offer a broad spectrum of investment management, estate planning, insurance, and tax advice. If you are looking for a generalist, a CFP may be perfect for you. In my opinion, someone who tries to be a generalist in the financial arena is, as the saying goes, a jack of all trades but a master of none. And when it comes to something as important as your financial future, you ought to get someone who's exceptionally proficient—a master.

Interview them. Don't be afraid to ask questions. After all, the adviser or broker sitting in front of you will be handling your hard-earned money. When you meet with an adviser for the first time, ask him how he gets paid, what training he has had, and what he specializes in. Quiz him about how he picks mutual funds and other investments. Beyond a good sales pitch, he needs to point to a rigorous process for how he evaluates investments and provides ongoing monitoring of those funds.

One other thing: Any broker or financial adviser can recommend a couple of decent mutual funds, but how many of these investment wizards take the time to counsel their clients about tax implications? Far too few. And that's just not right, because mutual funds, for all their investing advantages, can pose a tax headache for the novice investor.

It's also important to ask them about what you can expect from the relationship. How often will the adviser review your portfolio? Will she inform you when she does so? Will she make changes to your portfolio, or call you and ask first? How often will she communicate with you—will she call or email you? These answers can help you establish your expectations and trust.

Ask for referrals. Talk to friends, attorneys, or accountants about who they have chosen to be their adviser and why. Ask them about their experience with the adviser and whether they are happy with their adviser's investment choices and their portfolio's performance. Even then, bear in mind what I've already discussed—that the adviser should hold legitimate credentials and specialize in your area of need.

You can also ask your tax preparer. But if the CPA refers you to the financial planning department at his firm, be careful. When someone makes an internal referral, ask yourself whether it's because that referral is best for you or best for the company.

You could ask a potential adviser for the names of three or four clients, in hopes of asking them how satisfied they are. But I doubt this would be much help. First, client privacy is paramount in this business. It amazes me that people will openly discuss family troubles and their most intimate health problems, but even best friends rarely divulge how much money they have. As a result, we are convinced we have to keep everything very private.

What's more, even if an adviser does get clearance from a few clients who are willing to talk about their experiences, do you think they'll say anything negative? The adviser will steer you to only those clients he knows adore him.

Review the adviser's disciplinary and employment history. As you consider potential brokers and financial advisers, it probably wouldn't hurt to review their disciplinary and employment histories. Here's how to go about it:

- If it's an investment adviser you're researching, check out the SEC's Investment Adviser Public Disclosure website (www.adviserinfo .sec.gov).

- You can also request a copy of the adviser's disclosure brochure (Form ADV, Part II).

- For broker-dealers, go to the "BrokerCheck" section of the Financial Industry Regulatory Authority website (www.finra.org). The SEC and FINRA sites should show an individual's industry experience and whether he's been sued, fined, or barred from the industry. It's a permanent record. A single lawsuit isn't necessarily bad, but a whole bunch of lawsuits is probably a bad sign.

- You also might check with the Securities Commissioner's office for your state. Most have a Freedom of Information statute, which lets you request information on broker-dealers and financial advisers licensed in your state.

How to Work with a Financial Adviser

Once you have found the right adviser for you, discuss with the adviser your expectations about how often he or she will communicate and how and when the adviser will make changes to your portfolio. The biggest complaint I hear from people who have left a financial adviser is lack of communication. The client grumbles, "I changed jobs, had a rollover, and the guy sold me some mutual fund. That was four years ago, and it's the last time I've heard from him. He hasn't made any changes to my portfolio. The only time I talk to him is when I call him." The client understandably feels like a lost puppy. He's received little attention, and therefore his investments suffer.

It's not entirely the adviser's fault. The real culprit is the way the system is set up. As I've mentioned, most brokers work on commission, and that system lends itself to bad communication. When I was a commissioned broker, if I could sell you something today, I got paid today. Let's say you change jobs. You tell me you've got a $100,000 rollover, and that's all the money you have. So I sell you some mutual fund that has a 5-percent load, and I get a $5,000 commission.

Now, you've already told me that's all the money you have, and I need a paycheck next week, too, so what do I do? As a commissioned broker, I'd spend the preponderance of my day like a lion hunting for my next meal, looking for other people to sell to. That leaves me very little time during the day to step back and review your account.

So, what level of communication can you reasonably expect from your adviser? You should receive a personalized outbound communication—a call or an email, not just a glossy newsletter—at least twice a year. For example, at The Mutual Fund Store we have software that lets us look at our client accounts every day to ensure that each one is allocated properly. Then, at least twice a year every client gets an email or a call from the adviser, saying, "Here's the account today and everything looks in order." Or "We're reducing the amount of small caps and increasing large caps." Or "We're going to sell this fund and buy that fund."

Once a year, the adviser also needs to ask about the client's attitude toward risk: "I just wanted to check to see how you're doing. Is there any change in your life, or anything we need to know about that might prompt us to adjust the allocation?"

That's outbound communication. When the client calls her adviser, she should get a call back within one business day.

The other reason many people change advisers, of course, is that their investments haven't performed as they expect. That's why you need benchmarks. It's one thing to say your baseball team scored four runs last night. Is that good? Depends on what the other team scored. Sometimes four is good, sometimes not.

Surprisingly, some of the biggest names in the brokerage world—UBS, Morgan Stanley, Smith Barney—don't provide performance benchmarks in their customer statements. Their most elaborate statement for their biggest clients tells what the client owns, how much the client paid for it, and what it's worth now. That's not nearly enough context. The client learns he's earned, say, 40 percent on his investment, but what if it took ten years to get there? Suddenly 40-percent growth doesn't seem so hot. And what if a benchmark, like the S&P 500 Index, doubled during those ten years?

Even worse are statements that show only your individual position, or what you own now. Let's say you invested $10,000 and sold it for $8,000, then invested that $8,000 in something else. Now the statement shows your basis at $8,000, as if that's your starting point. Um, what happened to the $10,000?

Advisers should be accountable and their statements comparative. In the statements we send every quarter, for instance, we show the account's percentage change, the dollar return, *and* the performance of relevant benchmarks. We compare our client accounts to a benchmark that is relevant to the asset allocation of their particular portfolio. This way the client can see a similar comparison and also see how other asset allocation portfolios would have done.

Your efforts to proactively monitor and oversee your investments do not end once you have found a highly competent adviser, ascertained how he or she is paid, and entered into a relationship. With your new partner, you must thoughtfully and deliberately devise and implement a robust, rational plan. That is the focus of the next chapter.

HAVE A PLAN

Doctors don't start surgery without a plan. Not only do they decide what to do at each step in the procedure, but they also have contingencies in case the need should arise.

GREAT ACCOMPLISHMENTS almost always require a plan. When you are going to build a house, you don't just start hammering boards together until it looks like a house. When you need to have your appendix removed, the surgeon will have a plan. If something unexpected arises, he will deal with it and then go back to completing the plan. The same thing is true with your investments: you must have an all-encompassing plan, a strategy, an evolving blueprint.

Most investors, however, have no inkling of a plan. Typically, they make many uncoordinated efforts to accumulate investments over a period of time—without considering how those decisions may affect their financial future. That's just not good enough—particularly in today's high-risk, fast-changing world.

For example, a person might see an article in a magazine about a stellar-performing mutual fund. He pulls $10,000 from a checking account and rushes to buy $10,000 of that mutual fund. Then a few months later a broker calls with an exclusive tip (that he and dozens of other brokers are pushing to hundreds of clients). The investor now takes $5,000 from the checking account and buys $5,000 worth of shares in that stock. The question is, why did the investor put $10,000 in the mutual fund and $5,000 in the stock? Was it a strategic decision? No. It was an unplanned response. It's like buying a car one part at a time.

Over a period of time most investors—way too many investors— make a variety of investments and they end up with pools of money all over the place. They have no cohesive strategy. That's why it's important to develop a financial plan and stick to it. Keep in mind the following steps as you construct your plan:

- Establish your investment goals. Everyone should be investing for retirement—this is your first priority, once you have paid down bad debt and established your rainy-day fund. You may also have other needs, like buying a home, starting a business, or funding a college education.

- Diversify your investments. Asset allocation is essential. Mixing it up among different kinds of mutual funds is a good thing!

- Always keep an eye on how much volatility you can handle in your portfolio, and make sure your portfolio reflects your current circumstances (such as employment and marital status) and the economic environment.

- Don't plan just once. You need to revisit your plan again—and again.

Establish Your Investment Goals

To build a plan, you have to know your overarching personal goal. You should identify each of your goals, but realize that if it's a goal that's many years away, such as retirement, your plan to reach that goal may not produce the precise results that you initially plan.

For example, a thirty-year-old should have a goal of accumulating money for retirement. You can set up a plan to generate $4,000 a month of investment income thirty-five years from now—but that might not work, given market fluctuations and other unforeseen events over this long time horizon. There are just too many variables, and you would have to make too many assumptions. However, we can make some limited assumptions and deploy reasonable strategies—and then make adjustments along the way. The closer you get to your goal, the more precise you can be.

Suppose you plan a road trip from New York to Los Angeles to visit a friend or relative. When you leave New York, you don't need precise directions; you can just travel south and west, because there are many routes you can take. But once you get close to LA, you're going to need to know which exit to take from the freeway and street-by-street directions.

It's the same for retirement: the further away you are from your goal, the less precise you need to be. If your portfolio suffers during a setback in the market and you have many years to reach your destination, or goal, you have plenty of time to make it up. You can contribute more to your plan and ideally you'll earn bigger returns down the road. But as you get closer to retirement, you have to be more precise about what your needs are, and your options are more limited.

That's why your time horizon is important when you're defining your goals. If somebody is thirty-five years away from retirement, my advice to that person is, "Save as much as you can!" If you are ten to fifteen years away from retirement, then we need to look at very specific income numbers. Is the income you feel you'll need at that time even feasible, or do you need to save more each month?

Let's consider a hypothetical situation in some detail. Say your goal fifteen years from now is to have income of $5,000 per month. We can project how much your Social Security benefit will be. Let's say it is $1,200 a month. So now we know you need to come up with another $3,800 a month. To make that work, we might conclude that you will need to accumulate investments amounting to $700,000 in fifteen years. That triggers a whole new set of determinations: in the coming years, how is that money going to be invested and at what rate of return? We also have to make some assumptions about inflation. To what extent is your buying power going to erode? And when you start drawing income from savings, will it come from interest and dividends on the investments, or will you be taking out principal as well? In short, will the $700,000 be enough, and if not, how much more money will you need to contribute each month to your investment portfolio? Now we are getting closer to establishing a plan, a blueprint for ultimately achieving $5,000 a month in income.

Here are some guidelines for defining your investment goals:

1. Identify your financial goals and estimate the amount of money you need to accumulate to fulfill them.

2. Establish a time horizon or deadline. Do you need the investment income in five years or fifteen?

3. Make sure the goal is achievable. Sure, it would be nice to have a portfolio worth $1 million in five years, but this may not be realistic. There are many variables that could make some goals hard to achieve.

4. Prioritize your goals. Your first priority is to save for your own retirement. Other goals, such as saving for your children's education, should come after your retirement savings are

adequately funded. In other words, if you have money left over after contributing to your retirement accounts each month, that money can go toward your other goals.

Diversify Your Investments

Once you have established your goals, you're ready to start developing your strategy and picking investments for your financial plan. One of the most important strategies for your plan is to be diversified among many asset classes. This means you should have an appropriate mix of different kinds of stocks, fixed income, and cash, according to your tolerance for volatility—that is, swings in the value of your portfolio. Owning too much of any security increases the risk in your portfolio and could hurt your returns if that security loses value.

I have a client who had all of his portfolio in gold because he had had great returns over the past few years. This is sort of like selling crack—you can make great money at that too, but at some point you are going to go to jail and lose everything. Just because you have reaped returns from something for some time does not mean it's a good long-term strategy.

Asset allocation is key. The appropriate mix of stocks, bonds, and cash is different for everyone. Many mutual fund companies recommend certain allocations for people with various risk tolerances—typically a range of aggressive, moderate, and conservative—but there really are no set rules. Each of us must determine the exposure that we're comfortable with and also consider the time horizon for each goal.

If you're setting up your plan on your own, without a financial adviser, you can find the general recommended asset allocations and interactive tools on many fund companies' and financial websites. Setting up your allocation by yourself is certainly better than not doing it at all.

When it comes to setting up your asset allocation, though, I think hiring a qualified adviser adds value to most people's financial situation in excess of what that adviser charges. That's because your adviser will determine the right investments for each of your goals and should be checking your portfolio every quarter or so to make sure you have the right asset allocation. This is especially important when the market is volatile. You might not have the time to examine all of your holdings and decide which investments to sell and then find new ones to buy. In the long run, it's better to let an adviser do this work for you. Think of it this way: I'm in good shape, but I go to the doctor every year for a checkup just to make sure there are no problems.

The first step to take when setting up your asset allocation is to decide how much of your portfolio should be invested in stocks, fixed income such as corporate and municipal bonds, and cash-type securities such as CDs, money market funds, and Treasury bills. This depends on your time horizon for each goal and how much volatility you can stand, as well as the current and forecast economic conditions. In general, stocks are considered the growth part of your asset allocation; fixed income and cash-type investments are considered safer and provide more stable income over time.

How can you determine how much money to put into each asset? One common rule of thumb seen in many financial publications is that your allocation to fixed income should equal your age. So if you are forty years old, you should have 40 percent of your portfolio in fixed income investments.

I think this age rule is a bunch of hooey. I'll tell you why. If a fifty-year-old person comes to us and hasn't saved properly for retirement, she will have to allocate more money to stocks because she will need to generate higher returns to boost her nest egg before she reaches retirement age. On the other hand, if a thirty-five-year-old person has won the lottery and has $2 million to invest, we might be *more* conservative than we would normally be, because that person does not need to take more risk to get to where he needs to be. Essentially, each person has different goals and circumstances and risk tolerance, so an individual's asset allocation should be carefully crafted around that person's specific needs; it should not follow any kind of general rule.

When you have determined how much of your money you want to invest in stocks and how much risk you want to take, then you can pick the different types in this class that will fit your needs. Stocks are categorized as *growth* (this means the company's earnings and/or revenue

The Callan Periodic Table of Investment Returns

Annual Returns for Key Indices (1988–2007) Ranked in Order of Performance

1988	1989	1990	1991	1992	1993	1994	1995	1996	1997	1998	1999	2000	2001	2002	2003	2004	2005	2006	2007
Russell 2000 Value 29.47%	S&P/Citi 500 Growth 36.40%	LB Agg 8.96%	Russell 2000 Growth 51.18%	Russell 2000 Value 29.15%	MSCI EAFE 32.57%	MSCI EAFE 7.78%	S&P/Citi 500 Growth 38.13%	S&P/Citi 500 Growth 23.97%	S&P/Citi 500 Growth 36.52%	S&P/Citi 500 Growth 42.16%	Russell 2000 Growth 43.09%	Russell 2000 Value 22.83%	Russell 2000 Value 14.02%	LB Agg 10.26%	Russell 2000 Growth 48.54%	Russell 2000 Value 22.25%	MSCI EAFE 13.54%	MSCI EAFE 26.34%	MSCI EAFE 11.17%
MSCI EAFE 28.26%	S&P 500 31.69%	S&P/Citi 500 Growth 0.20%	Russell 2000 46.05%	Russell 2000 18.42%	Russell 2000 Value 23.86%	S&P/Citi 500 Growth 3.14%	S&P 500 37.58%	S&P 500 22.96%	S&P 500 33.36%	S&P 500 28.58%	S&P/Citi 500 Growth 28.25%	LB Agg 11.63%	LB Agg 8.43%	Russell 2000 Value -11.43%	Russell 2000 47.25%	MSCI EAFE 20.25%	S&P/Citi 500 Value 5.82%	Russell 2000 Value 23.48%	S&P/Citi 500 Growth 9.13%
Russell 2000 24.89%	S&P/Citi 500 Value 26.13%	S&P 500 -3.11%	S&P/Citi 500 Growth 41.70%	S&P/Citi 500 Value 10.52%	Russell 2000 18.89%	S&P 500 1.32%	S&P/Citi 500 Value 36.99%	S&P/Citi 500 Value 22.00%	Russell 2000 Value 31.78%	MSCI EAFE 20.00%	MSCI EAFE 26.96%	S&P/Citi 500 Value 6.08%	Russell 2000 2.49%	MSCI EAFE -15.94%	Russell 2000 Value 46.03%	Russell 2000 18.33%	S&P 500 4.91%	S&P/Citi 500 Value 20.81%	Russell 2000 Growth 7.05%
S&P/Citi 500 Value 21.67%	Russell 2000 Growth 20.16%	S&P/Citi 500 Value -6.85%	S&P/Citi 500 Value 38.37%	Russell 2000 Growth 7.77%	Russell 2000 Growth 18.61%	S&P/Citi 500 Value -0.64%	Russell 2000 Growth 31.04%	Russell 2000 Value 21.37%	S&P/Citi 500 Value 29.98%	S&P/Citi 500 Value 14.65%	Russell 2000 21.26%	Russell 2000 -3.02%	Russell 2000 Growth -9.23%	Russell 2000 -20.48%	MSCI EAFE 38.59%	S&P/Citi 500 Value 15.71%	Russell 2000 Value 4.71%	Russell 2000 18.37%	LB Agg 6.97%
Russell 2000 Growth 20.38%	Russell 2000 16.25%	Russell 2000 Growth -17.42%	Russell 2000 Value 30.47%	S&P 500 7.62%	S&P/Citi 500 Value 13.37%	Russell 2000 Value -1.55%	Russell 2000 28.44%	Russell 2000 16.53%	Russell 2000 22.36%	LB Agg 8.70%	S&P 500 21.04%	S&P 500 -9.11%	S&P/Citi 500 Value -11.71%	S&P/Citi 500 Value -20.85%	S&P/Citi 500 Value 31.79%	Russell 2000 Growth 14.31%	Russell 2000 4.55%	S&P 500 15.79%	S&P 500 5.49%
S&P 500 16.61%	Russell 2000 Value 14.53%	Russell 2000 -19.50%	S&P 500 22.56%	LB Agg 7.40%	S&P 500 10.08%	Russell 2000 -1.81%	Russell 2000 Value 25.75%	Russell 2000 Growth 11.32%	Russell 2000 Growth 12.93%	Russell 2000 Growth 1.23%	S&P/Citi 500 Value 12.73%	MSCI EAFE -14.17%	S&P 500 -11.89%	S&P 500 -22.10%	S&P 500 28.68%	S&P 500 10.88%	Russell 2000 Growth 4.15%	Russell 2000 Growth 13.35%	S&P/Citi 500 Value 1.99%
S&P/Citi 500 Growth 11.95%	LB Agg 12.43%	Russell 2000 Value -21.77%	LB Agg 16.00%	S&P/Citi 500 Growth 5.06%	LB Agg 9.75%	Russell 2000 Growth -2.44%	LB Agg 18.46%	MSCI EAFE 6.05%	LB Agg 9.64%	Russell 2000 -2.55%	LB Agg -0.82%	S&P/Citi 500 Growth -22.08%	S&P/Citi 500 Growth -12.73%	S&P/Citi 500 Growth -23.59%	S&P/Citi 500 Growth 25.66%	S&P/Citi 500 Growth 6.13%	S&P/Citi 500 Growth 4.00%	S&P/Citi 500 Growth 11.01%	Russell 2000 -1.57%
LB Agg 7.89%	MSCI EAFE 10.53%	MSCI EAFE -23.45%	MSCI EAFE 12.14%	MSCI EAFE -12.18%	S&P/Citi 500 Growth 1.68%	LB Agg -2.92%	MSCI EAFE 11.21%	LB Agg 3.64%	MSCI EAFE 1.78%	Russell 2000 Value -6.45%	Russell 2000 Value -1.49%	Russell 2000 Growth -22.43%	MSCI EAFE -21.44%	Russell 2000 Growth -30.26%	LB Agg 4.10%	LB Agg 4.34%	LB Agg 2.43%	LB Agg 4.33%	Russell 2000 Value -9.78%

○ **S&P 500 Index** measures the performance of large-capitalization U.S. stocks. The S&P 500 is a market-value-weighted index of 500 stocks that are traded on the NYSE, AMEX, and NASDAQ. The weightings make each company's influence on the Index performance directly proportional to that company's market value.

○ **S&P/Citigroup 500 Growth** and ● **S&P/Citigroup 500 Value Indices** measure the performance of the growth and value styles of investing in large cap U.S. stocks. The indices are constructed by dividing the market capitalization of the S&P 500 Index into Growth and Value indices, using style "factors" to make the assignment. The Value index contains those S&P 500 securities with a greater-than-average value orientation, while the Growth index contains those securities with a greater-than-average growth orientation. The indices are market-capitalization-weighted. The constituent securities are NOT mutually exclusive.

● **Russell 2000 Index** measures the performance of small-capitalization U.S. stocks. The Russell 2000 is a market-value-weighted index of the 2,000 smallest stocks in the broad-market Russell 3000 Index. These securities are traded on the NYSE, AMEX, and NASDAQ.

● **Russell 2000 Value** and ● **Russell 2000 Growth Indices** measure the performance of the growth and value styles of investing in small cap U.S. stocks. The indices are constructed by dividing the market capitalization of the Russell 2000 Index into Growth and Value indices, using style "factors" to make the assignment. The Value index contains those Russell 2000 securities with a greater-than-average value orientation, while the Growth index contains those securities with a greater-than-average growth orientation. Securities in the Value index generally have lower price-to-book and price-earnings ratios than those in the Growth index. The constituent securities are NOT mutually exclusive.

○ **MSCI EAFE** is a Morgan Stanley Capital International Index that is designed to measure the performance of the developed stock markets of Europe, Australasia, and the Far East.

○ **LB Agg** is the Lehman Brothers Aggregate Bond Index. This index includes U.S. government, corporate, and mortgage-backed securities with maturities of at least one year.

growth is higher than the average growth rate for its industry and the market) or *value* (a stock that trades at a good price compared to earnings growth), *large* or *small* as measured by market value (capitalization), and *domestic* or *international*.

At The Mutual Fund Store, once a client has determined his asset allocation for each goal, we invest in mutual funds, rather than individual securities, to fit his model. We start by dividing the client's portfolio among these basic asset classes: large-capitalization stock mutual funds, small- or mid-capitalization equity funds, international equity funds, fixed income funds, bonds, and balanced funds (a mix of stocks and fixed income).

At the next level we add sector funds, which focus solely on one business sector such as technology or health care. The choice of a sector and of how much money we allocate to certain sectors both depend on current economic conditions. For example, in the five years or so prior to this writing, commodities have performed very well given the high demand for raw materials, which pushed up prices of oil and other metals and materials. However, in 2008 this sector pulled back as the economy has slowed. Sometimes cycles last a year, sometimes longer, pushing certain types of investments in and out of favor (see chart on page 56). Trying to guess daily market movements is an impossible task. That's why we want our clients to have exposure to a variety of sectors and adjust the weightings, or allocations, as the economic and earnings outlooks change. In this way, investors are not chasing the best market performers and are continually participating in positive cycles of any one asset class.

Make sure each of your investment accounts has the right asset allocation. You need to set up the proper accounts to hold your investments for each of your goals. Think of it like the different areas of your home: there's a laundry room for washing your clothes, a kitchen for cooking your meals, and the bedroom for sleeping. Each serves its own particular purpose. You wouldn't want to house your retirement savings in a taxable account or have it earn little interest in a savings account. Your nest egg should be stored in a tax-deferred account such as a 401(k), IRA, or Roth IRA plan. Here's a brief rundown of some of the plans that you can consider for retirement and education.

Retirement accounts. First, let's consider some places to house your retirement savings. If you're working, contribute the maximum amount of your salary that you can afford into your company's 401(k) plan, which lets you set aside tax-deferred income. Some companies will match your contribution up to a certain percentage. But you don't want to touch this money until you reach retirement age, because you'd have to pay a penalty.

You can also set up a traditional IRA or Roth IRA, which allows you to contribute a certain amount each year. In a traditional IRA, your contributions may be tax deductible, depending on your income and tax filing status. When you withdraw money from a traditional IRA at retirement age, that money will be subject to income taxes. If you withdraw money before age fifty-nine and a half, you will be subject to a 10-percent penalty, unless the money is used for expenses that do not incur a penalty, such as purchasing a first home, paying for higher education expenses, certain medical expenses, and if you become disabled.

A Roth IRA works differently: contributions are not tax deductible, and the withdrawals are not taxed. You should always consider a Roth IRA first, unless you do not qualify due to your salary. To qualify, a person filing her taxes as single must have an adjusted gross income of less than $99,000, and married couples must have less than $156,000 in combined annual income (according to 2008 IRS rules). If you earn more than those amounts, you may be able to contribute lower amounts of money to a Roth IRA (check the IRS's website, www.irs.gov, for updated information). A Roth IRA is better than a traditional IRA because your withdrawals after age fifty-nine and a half will not be taxed. So you'll give up the tax savings on the income you contribute to a Roth IRA, but you'll have a larger benefit when you make withdrawals in your retirement years.

Education accounts. If you're saving for your children's education, you have plenty of accounts to choose from. These 529 plans are state-sponsored, with each state offering its own 529 version—similar to each other in many ways, but with enough cumbersome differences and varying fees to require extra homework before buying. By the way, for all you trivia buffs out there, the 529 designation—like the 401(k)—refers to the section of the IRS code that enables these savings programs.

On the surface, these 529 plans are a very sweet deal. The money you invest grows tax deferred. No federal tax. No state tax. That means you don't have to pay capital gains or income tax on earnings, as long as you use that money for college or any other qualified higher education, including trade schools. Some states even give an income tax credit for contributions to a 529. It's like they're paying you to invest!

However, there are some significant disadvantages to 529 plans. First, the investment options offered in these plans tend to be very conservative. Even the most aggressive funds in these plans are low growth compared to funds available in the market. Why? Remember, these are state-sponsored plans. Investment companies such as Vanguard often are selected to manage them, but it's the state treasurer whose job is on the line if the state's 529 falters. So treasurers deliberately limit 529 plans to options that are more conservative than you might choose on your own.

Likewise, when you invest in a 529 plan, typically you'll find just ten or fifteen fund choices. Compare that with more than 25,000 funds in my database. So now your choices aren't just conservative; you've also got only a handful from which to choose.

There's something else: you're allowed to switch investments just once a year in 529 plans, which limits your ability to be tactical. Some 529 programs also contain load funds. Their fees and expenses can be extremely high because the state is trying to make a profit. Those extra fees are kicked back to the state.

And then comes the real catch: If you withdraw the money for anything other than higher education, you not only have to pay income tax but also get nailed with a 10-percent federal penalty. That's just not right. You're hoping and planning that your child will go to college. But what if junior decides to start a business instead? One good thing is, you can change the beneficiaries of your plan.

There's an array of other programs to help you invest for your kids' college. You've probably heard of the Coverdell Education Savings Account (it used to be called an Education IRA). With a Coverdell, there's far more investment freedom—you can invest any way you want, and, much like the 529, the money grows tax deferred if it's used for higher education.

Coverdells also can be used to pay for certain elementary and secondary education (think private school), and even for academic tutoring.

Another sweet deal! With a Coverdell, however, you're limited to investing just $2,000 a year in the account. And just as with the 529 plan, you'll also pay taxes and a penalty if the money isn't used for qualified education.

However, a 529 ultimately lets *you* decide how the money gets spent, whereas a Coverdell requires that the funds be used to benefit the child (typically by age thirty), so you give up that control factor. You face income restrictions, too: if your adjusted gross income is more than $110,000 as a single tax filer or $220,000 as a married filer, you can't participate in a Coverdell.

Other college-saving options are the Uniform Gifts to Minor Act (UGMA) and the Uniform Transfers to Minor Act (UTMA), generally known as custodial accounts, which give you the freedom to invest much like a Coverdell—but without the annual $2,000 cap.

The catch? As with the Coverdell, not only must the money be used for the benefit of the child, but now the child may assume control of the account at the "age of majority," which is eighteen or twenty-one in most states. You want your teenagers to get their hands on that sort of cash? They'll show up in a Mustang convertible tomorrow, then head to Europe the day after.

The tax rules for custodial accounts can be cumbersome, too. The first $900 of earnings is tax free. Earnings between $900 and $1,800 are taxed at the child's rate, while earnings above $1,800 are taxed at the parents' rate. That's for children under age nineteen or until age twenty-three if the child is a full-time student. For children nineteen and over, all earnings are taxed at the child's rate. (These are 2008 limits and are subject to change.)

Choosing the right account can help you reach your financial goals. Remember, for each of these accounts that you set up, make sure you have the right asset allocation suited to each specific goal and time horizon.

Always Monitor Risk

Although many experts on Wall Street throw out terms like *risk* and *volatility* to describe the wild swings in the market from day to day, I prefer to think of volatility as how comfortable you are with fluctuations in your own investments. Essentially, no one is happy when she sees her portfolio lose value. In the late 1990s, investors were happy when the market was only going up. Then in 2000, when the market turned down and struggled for the next three years, people couldn't handle the risk and bailed.

People's appetite for volatility changes over time, so you periodically have to reevaluate your own. If you're rethinking what you're comfortable with, you should adjust your asset allocation. Make sure that as you get closer to your goal you dial down your risk.

Let's say your objective is that in fifteen years you will have $1 million. As you get three or four years away from reaching that $1 million target, you probably want to have a portfolio that's going to have less volatility so that you don't risk losing the handsome nest egg you have worked so hard to accumulate.

My core philosophy is that if you are going to take the risk of the market, you owe it to yourself to be in the best investments possible. No matter what your goal may be, my experience has convinced me that mutual funds are the investment vehicle of choice. Whether you own a good fund or bad fund, there is market risk. If the stock market goes down, both the bad fund and the good fund go down in value. The difference is that in good markets a good fund generally goes up more than a poor fund does. And in a bad market, the good fund generally declines less in value than a poor fund does. If we can make more in the good times and lose less in the bad times, the average returns will be very good. This represents a consistency of performance that should be treasured. The same thing holds true for bond funds. There are a lot of funds out there with similar risk parameters, but there are some managers who are consistently just better performers than others.

Plan Once . . . and Plan Again

Now that you have set your goals and determined your asset allocation and volatility tolerance, don't forget about your investments. You shouldn't treat your portfolio like it's a fancy dress or suit that you once wore to a formal affair and now hangs in your closet collecting dust. You

Target Allocations

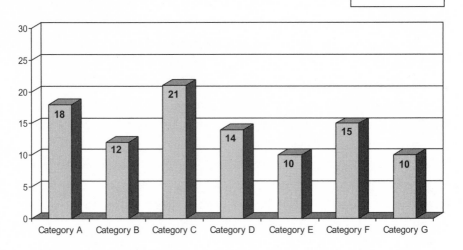

Target versus Actual Allocations

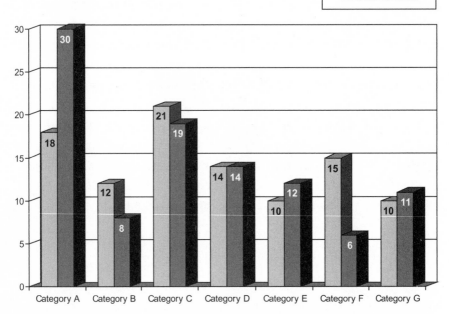

have to monitor and take care of your investments on a regular basis. If you nurture them, they will grow.

I think a quarterly review of your portfolio is appropriate for most people. Maybe twice a year is okay depending on the size of your portfolio. But any less often than that is neglecting your investments. After that evaluation, you need to determine whether rebalancing is necessary if your portfolio strays too far from your target allocation.

This applies to all of your investments—not only your taxable accounts. Your 401(k) needs just as much attention. Once you determine proper allocation percentages for *all* your accounts, you need to rebalance to be aligned with that target until market conditions or your needs dictate a new allocation.

On the previous page are two charts to illustrate how a plan can get out of balance from your target allocations. You can see this investor's target allocation—18 percent in category A, 12 percent in category B and so on. The next chart shows how fund performance and maybe the investor's contributions have caused the actual allocations to differ significantly from the target allocation for several categories.

Some investors, when they see this chart, focus on the categories that are underperforming. (We can see that several have drifted well below their target.) And then the investor gets excited about category A. It's really taken off! She thinks that category is hot, so maybe that's where she should be putting some new money.

Here's why you need to review and consider rebalancing on a regular schedule and stick to it. What about the categories that are down? If they represent a decreased percentage of the portfolio because it's an asset class that has declining prices, that's a buying opportunity.

And the category that's going gangbusters? It's exposing investors to increased risk. They originally targeted it to represent 18 percent of the portfolio, but it has grown so much it's now at 30 percent. If that category has a downturn, it's taking 30 percent of the portfolio with it.

With rebalancing, category A should be sold down to its target allocation of 18 percent. Those profits are used to make buys that bring the low categories back up to their targets.

When buying or selling, you want to be aware of any costs this activity might generate. For instance, in a taxable account, you don't want to sell a fund that just made a capital gains distribution and buy into one that's about to make one.

Here's another way of looking at it. Perhaps in 1996 you started out with a portfolio that was 50 percent stocks and 50 percent bonds. By the end of 1999, the portfolio may have been 80 percent stocks and 20 percent bonds. If you didn't do anything, you were slammed by the bear market of 2000, 2001, and 2002. After the stock market declines and the bull market for bonds, your entire "pie" would have shrunk and your portfolio might have been 70 percent bonds and 30 percent stocks.

On the other hand, if you and your adviser regularly rebalanced your portfolio to maintain 50 percent stocks and 50 percent bonds, the impact of the bear market would have been reduced and your average return over time would have been decent. Perhaps you wouldn't have made as much money in the good years, because in 1996 the market rose a lot. (There is no way to know in advance how things are going to work out.) As I write this book, the stock market is in a bear market. However, I am convinced that if you stick to your asset allocation and you periodically rebalance and reevaluate, you will win over time.

Some people use active rebalancing, making changes more frequently than every quarter. Obviously, this requires a lot of time and attention and might be best handled by a trained financial adviser. Whether you do your own investing or get help from an adviser, however, have the discipline to stick to your rebalancing schedule and make the changes that will keep you in line with your target allocation.

Putting Planning into Practice

Now that you know the four key steps to creating a solid investment plan, let me give you an example of how my wife and I went about crafting one investment plan: for our children's education fund. We followed the steps I've just outlined when we set out to plan for our children's education. First we established our goal—to be able to send our three children to college when they turn eighteen—and then we figured out what amount of money we needed to do so. We actually didn't have any amount per child in mind. In fact, we worked our way back into the numbers. First we figured how much we'll need to spend for ourselves in retirement, *then* we decided to put whatever was left into the college fund.

I'm hoping it's enough. But if it's not, remember my first rule about college savings plans: there are other options to fund a college education—scholarships, loans, the kids may have to work, or we can try to cover extra college costs from our monthly cash flow—so you should always save for your retirement first. I repeat, there's no scholarship for your retirement.

We also needed to have a time horizon and adjust our investment allocations accordingly. We started investing for our kids' college education when they were young, so we can be aggressive in our investment choices. After all, we've got a few more years to make up for any losses in our more daring choices. But we'll start throttling back on our risky ways two or three years before they start their college education, knowing we'll need to spend some of those funds in three years, some in four, five, and six years—and maybe even beyond to cover grad school. The worst that can happen with this approach is we'll get lower returns. I'm not suggesting I'll move all our college savings into CDs when our children turn fifteen. But as we monitor risk and we near our investment deadline, we do need to become progressively more conservative.

Regardless of what type of account we chose to house the college savings—529, Coverdell, traditional mutual funds, or something else—we have always monitored our investment plan periodically and made adjustments as necessary.

As you can see, setting up your financial plan is not easy. It takes time to figure out your asset allocation and risk tolerance and apply them to each goal, and then pick the right investments. And you have to be committed to your financial future—meaning, you must not neglect it and thereby put yourself at risk. If you don't have the time to do it, hire a professional adviser to help you craft the best possible plan. Ultimately, it is your responsibility to carefully plan for the future and engage professionals who can help you refine and execute your plan.

BE IN THE BEST FUNDS POSSIBLE

Participating in the markets means taking risks.
So if you're going to take the risk of the market,
why not be in the best funds possible?

ONCE YOU HAVE ESTABLISHED all of your goals and asset allocations, you're ready for the next step: choosing the best mutual funds. As I've said, it's my philosophy that mutual funds are the best way to achieve your financial goals. Mutual funds offer two very important advantages that you don't get by buying individual securities: professional management and diversification.

Professional management means that while you go to work, raise your children, and then keep busy by playing golf in your retirement years, there's someone working all day long and watching your mutual fund and deciding what to buy, sell, and hold. This fund manager is professionally trained to evaluate securities and is not emotionally attached to your money. And if you've chosen the fund properly, the manager has an established track record and is really good at it.

A mutual fund also provides diversification. For example, if you have $10,000 to invest, you might be able to buy five stocks. If one stock turns out to be Enron or Lehman Brothers or Bear Stearns, you're out of luck. It's very difficult for an investor to get properly diversified by buying individual securities, and it's also costly. On the other hand, a mutual fund will typically own thirty to more than one hundred stocks, so if one of them goes under, it won't be a disaster. The fund manager is making sure that the fund is not too heavily exposed to any one stock or sector.

There's one thing to keep in mind, though. Mutual funds have a very low entertainment value. If you watch CNBC, you'll see Jim Cramer screaming and throwing things when he talks about individual stocks. Mutual funds don't split their stock two-for-one, they don't have a blowout quarter for earnings, and they usually don't get acquired by other companies. If what you're after is entertainment, I'd say go to Vegas. If what you're after is real money for your retirement and other goals, mutual funds are the way to go.

The good news is there are plenty of mutual funds to choose from. A lot of people think they'll do fine simply by investing in mutual funds. After all, mutual funds by definition represent financial diversity. By pooling investments from many people and putting that money into stocks, bonds, and other securities, mutual funds represent a terrific investment choice, right? Not necessarily. Not all mutual funds were created equally. Bad funds rise in a good market—but not as high as a good fund does. And good funds decline in a bad market—but not as low as a bad fund does.

Picking the ones that will climb the most isn't so easy, however. Consider the investment community's most passionate refrain: "Past performance does not guarantee future results." Slapped at the end of practically every brochure, advertisement, and TV commercial that deals with investing, the disclaimer has become so ubiquitous it's like background noise. Yet there's no mistaking the upshot of this legal proviso. Even though a certain fund has increased, say, 140 percent over the past twelve years, don't assume for one moment it will earn you a dime once you put money into it. Got it?

Lawyers can wring all the fun out of life.

The irony is, past performance is *the single most important factor* when considering future results. In that way, the people who manage mutual funds are like athletes. Fund managers decide what to buy, what to sell, and when. If you track their performance through the years, you get a pretty good idea who the better ones are, and even how they might perform in different situations.

It reminds me of baseball. For every game situation, there are decades' worth of statistics that suggest how the play will go. A good coach knows that his lefty in the bullpen faces better odds against a left-handed hitter. And if the winning run is on second in the ninth, now the skipper is mentally chewing over stats about which relief pitcher stands a better chance of forcing the batter to hit to the left side of the field, perhaps keeping the runner at second.

The same wealth of statistics exists in investing—that's why I pore over research about mutual fund managers. If I see a manager who's beaten the market in one-, three-, five-, and ten-year time frames, someone who's been in the top 20 percent of all funds over that period, well, he's the guy I want to put in the game. There might be a dozen electrifying rookies on the bench, but you need to go with proven winners.

The strategy, ultimately, is about increasing your odds of winning. And more often than not the players and managers who have prevailed over the long haul will continue to succeed. Why invest in a middling fund led by an average manager when you can invest in the all-stars?

The beauty of mutual funds—compared with baseball—is that it really doesn't cost any more to own a good fund than it does to own a lousy one. There's only one Alex Rodriguez in real life, and the New York Yankees have him locked up, but when it comes to picking mutual funds, you and everyone else who plays can buy the A-Rod of funds and put him on your team.

There are no guarantees, of course. The lefty might give up a homer, A-Rod strikes out sometimes, and your all-star fund manager occasionally underperforms his peers. But based on their past performance, odds are good the players will indeed bring the results you want.

If you are going to take the risk of the markets, you owe it to yourself to be in the best investments possible. Next I'll explain how to choose mutual funds and some things to keep in mind while you're examining and weighing all of those choices.

Boring Is Beautiful

One day a caller to my radio show said he had received a letter about an investment opportunity. Apparently the Chinese government is planning to buy all the uranium in the world as a way to supply the country's demand for nuclear power, and the investment guru in this letter was advising a portfolio of uranium stocks.

That's a great story, isn't it? You can picture the voracious Chinese economy needing tons and tons of uranium to support its growing demand for electricity. That's Extreme Uranium. It's new and improved all over again.

It may sound like a good idea on paper, but is it? Rather than buying into a good story, I look for funds with consistent returns over many years and a fund manager who has been at the helm for a long time. There are funds like the Wasatch 1st Source Income Equity Fund, run by Ralph Shive. Over the past ten years, Ralph has beaten the S&P 500 by about 5 percentage points a year. If you take five times ten, that's fifty. Now compound it. That means if you had put $10,000 into the fund ten years ago, its current value would be more than one and a half times greater than the same investment in the S&P Index.

That's boring, right? There's no uranium. No voracious Chinese economy. Ralph's just a guy who's shown an ability over time to know which stocks to buy, how long to hold them, and when to sell. Even during the difficult period for the market in the fall of 2008, this fund's performance was still superior to that of the S&P 500.

His fund's success illustrates another boring fact: you don't necessarily need the big brands like Fidelity in your portfolio. Sure, Fidelity is a household name among investors, but some of the best funds are ones you've never heard of, such as Wasatch 1st Source Income Equity Fund. That's because they're not marketed heavily in the media.

Some of these little-known funds, such as Hodges Fund and Keeley, were created almost by accident. They're the by-product, so to speak, of institutional money managers who historically focused on the big fish— university endowments, pensions, and large corporations. The managers were so successful at these institutions that "friends of the institution," such as professors and alumnae, urged the managers to launch mutual funds in which the friends could invest their own money.

Now, these no-name funds are small potatoes compared with the institutional side of the managers' business—representing maybe 5 percent of their assets—thus, their lack of promotion. No matter. They're led by some of the best managers in the business, and you can buy them.

Wasatch 1st Source Income Equity Fund and the Hodges Fund and Keeley are just a few examples that prove that searching for fund managers with steady track records year after year can lead you to the best funds. You don't have to follow the latest trend or gimmick. Also, keep in mind that the big brands like Fidelity don't offer the best funds for every asset class. Focus on the tried and true—go with a manager who's shown an ability to do better most of the time.

How to Pick the Best Mutual Funds

You can find the best funds by searching for the fund managers who have the most consistent returns over a long time period. Don't chase the best-performing funds in any short time span such as one quarter or one year, because many of them can have strong returns in one short time period and then do poorly in the next. In other words, you should avoid the one-hit wonders. Usually, they are piling into the best-performing stocks or sector, and they run the risk of getting hit when those high fliers start to dive. And you should certainly not choose a fund just because it was featured in a personal finance magazine.

Another thing to consider: size matters. Avoid many popular funds with very large assets like Fidelity Magellan because their size can limit the amount of money that they can invest in their best stock ideas. At the gigantic Magellan fund, its rules allow it to buy a certain amount of each security. So if Magellan's manager thinks Joe's Company is his best idea, he can buy a limited number of Joe's shares. If there's money left over, he can invest in his second best idea, and so on. That's why many mutual funds with very large assets close off their funds to new investors—they just can't put money to work effectively. I prefer funds that are smaller in size, whose managers can be more flexible when investing in their best ideas.

Those are just a few things to keep in mind when considering a mutual fund. Here are a few steps you can take to select the best fund for yourself.

1. *Determine your asset allocation*. Before you choose your funds, decide what types of funds you want. As I said in chapter 4, it's essential that your investments contain a certain percentage of stocks and bonds, large cap and small cap, domestic and international. The actual percentage, or asset allocation, tells you what kind of funds to own, and in what proportions.

   A portfolio of seven to ten funds is ideal. Of course, the specific number of funds really depends on how much you have to invest. Just make sure that you don't put too much money in any one fund belonging to one asset class.

   Also check the fund's top holdings: you don't want to own two funds that hold the same stocks or securities. Remember, you want to always be both diversified and not too heavily exposed to any one security.

   If you're trying to decide between two different funds in one asset class, take a look at the risk of each fund. One way to measure a fund's risk or volatility is its beta, which indicates how a fund tends to react to swings in the market. If a fund has a beta of 1, this means that the fund's return tends to move with the market. A beta of less than 1 means that the fund is less volatile than the market; a beta greater than 1 shows that the fund is more volatile than the market. You can find a fund's beta on the fund's website or Morningstar.com. If one fund that you've chosen has a higher beta than the other, then you have to determine whether that extra risk is worth taking.

2. *Screen for consistency.* The next step is to decide on the specific funds you want by looking for consistent returns. You can use screening software to search for funds in each category and asset class with the highest returns over the past five years. I prefer to use the mutual fund screener provided by Morningstar.com—which offers side-by-side comparisons of funds from all different companies—rather than the online tools offered by a fund company, such as Fidelity, that wants to push its own funds. If you have a financial adviser, you can ask her to screen for the funds that will best suit your chosen asset allocation.

   Once you have a list of the funds with the highest average returns over the past five years in a specific asset class, you can narrow the list further by looking beyond the average return. Sometimes a fund will post one year of extraordinarily high returns. That makes the average look good—but it was really the manager getting lucky one year.

   To check for consistency, look at a fund's total returns provided by the fund company or the fund's profile on Morningstar.com. Compare the performance each year to the appropriate indexes. Morningstar provides performance data for the past eight years. How many times did the fund beat its benchmark? If the average returns are good but the fund beat the index only half the time, the performance is too hit or miss for my taste. On the other hand, if the fund topped the index at least six of the past eight years, it's a good candidate to buy.

Note that Morningstar shows the performance versus the index or benchmark as a "+/-." In other words, a fund with a 5.5 outperformed the index or benchmark by 5.5 percentage points that year. A -4.6 means it underperformed those peers by 4.6 percentage points.

You should also consider how the fund performed in good years (2003–04) versus bad ones (2000–02). Many do well during lush times but stink during a bear market. Others are more consistent—they post strong returns during the good times and lose less or even hold steady during the bad. Those are the types of funds you want to own.

Remember the disclosure "past performance doesn't guarantee future results." Past performance *does* matter. Consider Tiger Woods. When he leads a major golf tournament after two days, his past performance suggests his future outcome will be pretty darn good. The same goes for top mutual fund managers.

3. *Check the manager.* After you've found a fund that looks tempting, make sure the same manager who was responsible for the past performance is still calling the shots today. How? Fund companies will provide the number of years that the manager has been running the fund. You can also find a manager's tenure on Morningstar.com. Remember, any performance figures before the current skipper took charge are irrelevant, because someone else was picking investments for the fund.

   Sometimes a fund manager will leave his company for another job, or the company will switch a manager to run another one of its funds. If the name of the fund stays the same but the manager changes, it's not the same fund.

4. *Choose no-load funds.* Always, always pick a no-load fund over a fund that charges a load. There's no reason to pay a load. Remember, the load goes to the broker, not to the fund. It's his enticement for recommending that fund over another. The more you pay in fees, the less your portfolio will return in the long run. That means it will take longer for you to reach your goals.

Here's a simple way to illustrate it. Your car is running out of gasoline, so you need to find a station to fill it up. If one station nearby is selling a gallon of gas for $4 and another one across the street is selling it for $3, which one would you choose? Of course, the smart buyer would drive to the station across the street for the cheaper price so that the bill is lower.

Some people believe they have to pay more for something to get the best product on the market. That's not true for mutual funds. For any load fund that you find, you'll find a no-load fund that's just as good. If you choose no-load funds, you'll be richer down the road.

Picking the best fund is easier than ever now that investment research sites such as Morningstar.com allow almost anyone to check a fund's holdings, performance over time, and manager. But I believe that when it comes to finding the best fund, avoiding fees and hidden costs is so important that it deserves its own commandment. So read the next chapter to learn more about fees. You'll be glad you did.

AVOID *ANY* HIDDEN COSTS

Know what you're paying for. There's no need to pay commissions and loads when you can get funds that are just as good or better without paying a load.

WHEN YOU ARE ESTABLISHING your financial plan, pay attention to how much it's going to cost you. In the investment world, you should expect to pay a little more to get the best products and results. Often, you will find that you get what you pay for—meaning that if an investment costs less, it may not turn out to be the best product.

A good example is Pop-Tarts. Yes, those sweet, delicious toaster pastries. Would you pay more for a box of Pop-Tarts, or would you try to save a few pennies on your grocery bill by choosing the lower-priced store brand? They certainly look the same as pictured on the box, but I believe anyone who has eaten both will agree: Pop-Tarts are worth the extra cost. Pop-Tarts just taste better. So when it comes to saving for your financial future, don't choose an investment just because it costs less. That said, you also want to make sure that you're not paying *too much*.

It may seem a little overwhelming to pay attention to costs while you're also trying to choose among the thousands of investment products, where to house them, and how you're going to monitor your investments. But I can assure you, it's really not that difficult—you just need to know what the various costs are.

As you learn the ins and outs and become more comfortable with investing, you may become confident that you can manage your financial plan and all of the costs that come with it. However, if you've decided to hire a professional financial adviser to help you create and implement your plan, then as I've already stressed, a fee-based adviser usually offers the best value. As I discussed in chapter 3, the cost of a fee-based adviser depends on the dollar amount of your portfolio. Over time, as your portfolio rises in value, you'll be paying your adviser the same percentage but a larger sum of money because you are paying on a larger balance. Some advisers will reduce the percentage as your account reaches certain levels. But if your adviser is very good and you're successfully reaching your goals, the original percentage fee will be well worth it.

The cost of managing and implementing your plan should be easy to determine. But there are some hidden costs. The costs to look for typically come in two forms: fees and taxes. You will pay fees or loads when you buy mutual funds. I'll explain why loads are bad and why management fees are acceptable. The other cost is taxes. Yes, we all have to pay our dues to Uncle Sam, however there are strategies you can use to lessen your tax burden. First, let's take a look at loads and management fees.

Stay Away from Loads

A load is a commission that's charged by the broker who is selling a mutual fund. A common misperception is that the load is paid to the mutual fund—in fact, the payment actually goes to the broker. The load is the broker's enticement for selling the fund.

Why are loads bad? There are a lot of reasons. For one, when someone goes to a broker looking to invest his money, he's looking for help and advice. When you buy a load fund, the broker gets paid the commission up front. No matter how the investment performs, the broker gets paid the same amount.

I've said it before, but it bears repeating: as soon as you purchase that load fund, you're already losing money. So if you invest $10,000 in a load fund and the broker gets $500 in commission, you'll have $9,500 in your account. That fund has to rise in value by $500 just to get back to your $10,000 starting point. By paying that load, you also lose the compounded growth, which means it will take you longer to reach your investment goals.

Another reason I don't like loads: they can make you feel trapped in a bad investment. Let's say you've bought a load fund, and at some point market conditions change and the fund isn't performing as you thought it would. You want to sell it. If you switch to another fund outside of that fund family, you'll have to pay another load. If you don't want to pay another load, the broker will probably look for another fund in the same fund family. The problem is, staying in the same fund family limits your choices and your chances to find a better investment.

What's worse, a broker may sell you a fund and then simply forget about you because he wants to make more money by selling funds to someone else. This is how the commission-based broker system works. Brokers are not bad people; they're just salespeople—they have to make a living by selling as many funds and other investments as possible.

Load funds come in all shapes and sizes. When you're searching for mutual funds, you'll see many of them listed as A shares, B shares, and C shares. All of these share classes carry some type of load, so don't buy them. The A shares have a *front-end* load, which means the broker gets paid a commission up front when the broker initially sells the fund. The B shares have a *back-end* load (or deferred sales charge). If you sell B shares within five to seven years, you have to pay a penalty of 5 to 7 percent. And with B shares, the fund company pays the broker an up-front commission, but then you have to pay the fund company higher ongoing operating expenses. A mutual fund company usually charges an extra 1 percent a year more for operating expenses for the B shares than they would for A shares. The C shares will charge you a back-end load if you sell the fund within the first year, but it's typically only 1 percent. However, it will charge a higher management fee for ongoing operating expenses than you will pay for A shares. (The C shares also carry the same high expense ratio as the B shares.)

My company and some other fee-only advisers buy A shares with the load waived for our clients. So we get the lowest management fee class with no loads. This allows us to offer a wider selection of low-cost funds that individual investors might not have access to on their own. If you are searching for funds on your own, look on Morningstar.com and other financial websites that say "no load" where the fees and expenses are listed.

Another fee to watch for is 12b-1, which are marketing costs and distribution expenses that the fund company pays for. These fees are listed in the fund prospectus and on many financial websites. These are worth knowing about because if you buy a fund through an adviser or broker, the fund company may be paying that adviser, or providing sales incentives such as free trips, to sell that fund. In other words, the adviser may be placing you in that fund because he's getting that fee or incentive, not because the fund is right for your portfolio.

I know what some of you are thinking, "Adam sure likes to rag on load funds a bunch—but isn't a load basically just a big up-front fee for a mutual fund?" In that spirit, you're thinking, a load fund that dramatically outperforms a no-load is worth it. Well, that's true in theory but plain silly in reality. Show me any load fund and I can show you no-load funds that perform just as well or better.

Now that you've learned to stay away from loads, let's talk about the other fund fees that you should keep an eye on.

Don't Fret the Management Fees

Some investment gurus like to zero in on differences in mutual fund fees. A fund that charges lower fees clearly is a better choice, they argue. Before we get into this debate, let me explain which fees I'm talking about. I'm referring to the management fee, which is included in the fund's total operating expenses. This fee varies depending on the type of fund. Bond funds typically have lower management fees because their returns are lower. International equity funds have higher expenses because their managers have to travel all over the world to visit the companies in which they are investing.

Management fees are acceptable as long as the manager is giving you value for that fee. If the fund has a high management fee and its performance stinks, then it's a bad deal. But some funds with higher management fees are worth it. What I care about is the fund's net returns.

Truth is, higher management fees do create a larger performance hurdle for the fund manager to overcome, because their investments have to rise more in value to offset the management fee and make their clients whole. But a higher management fee doesn't mean that a fund manager can't make up the cost for her investors and beat the fund managers who charge less.

That's why you need to focus more on a fund's performance. Consider an index fund, with a 0.15 percent management fee, whose performance exactly mirrors the S&P 500. You're comparing it with, say, the Royce Low-Priced Stock Service (RYLPX), a mutual fund with a management fee of 1.49 percent. Over the past ten years (through December 2007), the Royce fund has returned an average of 14.2 percent per year, versus 5.8 percent for the index fund, net of fees.

Let's think about how that performance can add up, in that actual market period. If you had invested in the Royce Low-Priced Stock Service at the beginning of 1998, and left your investment there so that all your gains were reinvested to grow further, then ten years later, your original investment in our "high-priced" mutual fund would have grown a total of 277 percent, versus 74 percent for a cheap index fund, *even after accounting for fees.* So $10,000 invested in the Royce Low-Price Stock Service back at the start of 1998 would have grown to $37,670 by 2008, while the cheap index fund would have grown to less than half that: $17,625. By going with the Royce fund, even though it has higher expenses, your return would have been more than twice as high over the decade.

What if I had to choose between two funds with the same returns? I would take the fund with the lower expenses, because that manager will have a lower performance hurdle to overcome to achieve higher returns.

Remember, what matters is not what you pay the mutual fund company, but how much money you make by investing in their funds. The reported returns of a no-load mutual fund are net of all fees. I'm not talking about loads or commissions that go to a broker. I'm talking about the actual management fees that go to the fund company.

Go to Morningstar.com and see how long the manager has handled that fund, then look at the returns for that time period. If the manager has consistently beaten her peers with good returns, then she's earning whatever fees she's getting.

It's smart to be price conscious—just don't let fees drive your investment decisions.

Are Index Funds and ETFs Worth It?

Another great debate among investors is whether actively managed funds are better than index funds, which invest in the same stocks as a certain index and have much lower expenses. The proponents of index funds like to quote the statistic showing that 80 percent of actively managed funds perform worse than the S&P 500 Index and only 20 percent can beat the market.

I don't like index funds, because you know that you'll never do better than the index. If you do your homework, you can find the 20 percent of actively managed funds that have been able to beat the market over time. The alternative is to have an adviser do the homework for you. We have more than 25,000 funds in our database, and all you need to consider for yourself is seven to ten funds. I'm not saying that index funds are bad, but when you buy an index fund you're automatically accepting that index's performance. In other words, you're missing out on the greater potential returns that active fund management can bring.

The same goes for exchange-traded funds (ETFs), which have become very popular. ETFs are simply index funds that trade like stocks all day long. The industry is portraying ETFs as if they are a whole separate asset class. But the F in ETF stands for fund!

If you're a day trader, ETFs are great because you can buy and sell them when the market is open. But most people aren't day traders, so all they're getting is an index fund, and because it's traded like a stock, they have to pay a commission to buy and sell it.

Mutual fund companies have been marketing ETFs very heavily and have been successful selling them. But that's not because ETFs are a great new investment.

In the long run, even though it may cost a little more, you have a better chance of generating higher returns from an actively managed no-load mutual fund.

Keep a Lid on Tax Costs

As I've said many times, mutual funds are wonderful investment vehicles, but when it comes to taxes they can make your head spin if you're not familiar with how they work. This is particularly important to know if your funds are in a taxable account.

Here's why: Mutual fund companies don't pay taxes. As they buy and sell individual stocks and bonds and generate a profit or pay dividends or interest, the fund companies *distribute* those payments and capital gains to shareholders—investors like you—in a pro rata portion each year.

Most mutual funds' fiscal year ends on October 31. During November they compute their capital gains distributions, and they usually pay them out in December. If you invest in a mutual fund in July and, for whatever reason, sell it in December, you may still receive a taxable distribution from it, because you were a "shareholder of record." You'll face the same tax hit whether you own the fund for a day, a year, or five years.

Don't get caught in this tax trap! And you definitely want to avoid the double whammy of selling a fund that's just made its distribution, then jumping into one that's about to do it. Most funds have this information on their websites, or you can check with your financial adviser to make sure your timing is prudent.

With our clients, we contact the fund companies by mid-November to determine what distributions they expect. If the record date is in early December, with the distributions sent one or two weeks later, there's still time to make a decision in mid-November about how to proceed.

Let's say you invested $10,000 in a large cap value fund in June and the market languishes over the next couple of months, so by November 15 your investment is still worth just $10,000. After contacting the fund company, we discover the firm anticipates a 15-percent capital gains distribution. If you do nothing, you'll receive a 1099 form from the fund company, obligating you to pay taxes on that $1,500 distribution—even though you didn't reap that gain.

Ouch. You're better off selling the fund immediately, before the record date of distribution in early December. Why? Rather than face those taxes, it makes more sense to sell a fund you've owned for a short period at a loss. Or if the gains are substantially less than what the mutual fund company's distributions will be, you can sell the fund so there's no tax liability, then shift the investment into another large cap value fund that won't have a big distribution.

You can "harvest" your losses, too. Let's say you bought a fund for $10,000 five years ago, and now it's worth $20,000. That's great, but the bad news is the fund will have a $1,500 distribution this year. You still like the fund, and if you sell it you'll face more tax liability, so what else can you do? Let's say you also bought a fund in June of this year for $10,000, and now it's at $9,000. You can sell it at $9,000, immediately invest the proceeds in another fund, and use that $1,000 loss to offset gains you'll face from the first fund. The net-net of this loss harvesting: taxes on $500 rather than on $1,500.

Keep in mind that there is a "wash sale" rule. The wash sale rule prevents you from claiming a loss on a sale of a stock or a mutual fund if you buy the same stock or fund within the thirty days before or after the sale. For example, if you sell a mutual fund, you would not want to buy the same fund within a thirty-day period.

During the bear market in the first years of the twenty-first century, we advised clients to sell a lot of funds, even though we liked the investments. We expected the market to rebound, and we knew we could carry the losses forward. The solution? Sell the funds at a loss and put those proceeds into other funds, knowing we could use those losses to offset taxes on future gains.

Some funds have a history of high tax distributions. You can check them out at the Morningstar website. Look up a fund, then click on the "tax analysis" tab at the left. That will show you its "tax cost ratio" covering the past one, three, and five years. For example, a fund with a pretax return of 15 percent and an after-tax of 13 percent has a tax cost ratio of about 2 percent a year. (The formula is actually more complex, but this gives you a rough idea.)

Fund tax costs, which vary substantially, are related to the amount of trading, or turnover, done by the fund manager. High turnover and tax cost aren't necessarily a sign of a bad fund. It can be a valid strategy, in fact. The key to investing in those funds is to put them in your IRA or other retirement account; for your taxable account, lean toward funds with better tax efficiencies.

Some clients don't want to sell a fund at all because they're fearful of the tax consequences. A radio caller said she's owned a mutual fund for ten years. For the first seven it was a solid investment, returning about 10 percent a year, but since then it's stagnated, barely keeping up with inflation. Time to sell, I suggested.

"Oh no!" she responded. "I'll have to pay taxes on the gains."

Well, yeah, but you need to give only *some* of the gains to the government; you'll put the rest in a different fund, where there's more opportunity for *additional* gains. Taxes are never—*never!*—a reason not to sell something. Holding on to the old fund is like refusing to cash in a winning lottery ticket because you don't want to pay taxes on your millions. We saw it a lot during the go-go nineties—investors, fearful of the tax hit, decided to stick with their high-tech stocks. Needless to say, they wound up giving those gains back to the market.

Consider Hiring a Good CPA

Personally, I don't mind paying taxes. We live in an incredible country where you can get in your car and drive just about anywhere without asking permission. Practice any religion. Get artichokes in the middle of winter. For those and a thousand other reasons, I'm happy to pay my dues.

Having said that, no one wants to overpay Uncle Sam. I see clients frequently doing their own taxes, and I respect their gumption. Just because they can do the computations, however, doesn't mean they understand the intricacies of tax law. I wonder how many dollars they're giving up to save a few pennies.

In other words, for folks who are building notable wealth—not multimillion-dollar fortunes, mind you, but healthy investment port-folios—I suspect the fee you'd pay to a *competent* tax preparer would be worth the savings. That fee will vary substantially, of course, based on the complexity of the return, but figure on $350 to $500 as a ballpark estimate for someone who's investing primarily in mutual funds.

To me that's money well spent. Otherwise it's so easy to miss deduc-tions. Consider this situation: Clients of The Mutual Fund Store pay investment management fees, which are deductible on a taxable account. Typically we debit that fee from the account. If we take the manage-ment fee from an IRA account, it's not deductible. Thus you're better off paying the IRA fee directly, or having your taxable account debited. Doing so saves you roughly a third on your fees, depending on your tax bracket.

That's an example of one of the many little things investors miss on their taxes. Another common slip involves the alternative minimum tax (AMT). The AMT was created in the 1970s to force wealthy people to pay their fair share. At the time, some of them were putting all their money into tax-free bonds. Think $20 million invested in 5-percent bonds. That earned them a cool $1 million a year in income—and no income taxes.

So Congress devised the AMT as a way to counter such strategies. The tax included a person's capital gains, income from tax-free muni bonds, and itemized deductions, among other factors. Problem was, the tax wasn't indexed to inflation. When it was first enacted it affected fewer than 1 percent of the population. By 2010, however, the Congressional Budget Office estimates that one in five taxpayers will be liable— essentially every married taxpayer with income of $100,000 or more. Over the past few years, Congress has issued a protective patch but has not yet passed a permanent solution.

All of which means the AMT must be considered in your investment decisions. Selling some mutual funds this year, rather than waiting, may very well bump you into the AMT bracket and trigger 13 percent more tax on every dollar of income. That's where a good CPA comes in handy. Be sure to meet with your CPA early in the tax cycle, when you can still make adjustments—not in January, when it's too late.

Finally, as I write this book, the long-term federal capital gains (defined as any security owned for at least twelve months) of 15 percent max is slated to expire at the end of 2010. You want to make sure any gains in your taxable accounts are capital gains—that's probably the lowest tax rate you'll ever pay.

And if Congress doesn't act? That means gains on any securities sold starting in 2011 will be taxed at your nominal income rate, which could be 30 percent or more. If that's the case, plan on getting busy in late 2010 selling and harvesting as many of those gains as you can.

On the other hand, if such tax language gives you the creeps, call in a good CPA. He'll earn his keep.

Now that you have a good handle on costs and how to avoid them, it's time to make sure you understand the investments that you're buying.

DON'T BUY WHAT YOU DON'T UNDERSTAND

If you react emotionally to the markets, you are going to buy and sell the wrong things at the wrong time.

IN LATE 2008 IT WAS REVEALED that a New York-based investment adviser, Bernard Madoff, had swindled investors out of what he reported to be $50 billion. While I have great empathy for those who lost money in his scheme, there were many warning signs that should have tipped off those investors that something was amiss.

I certainly hope that you never run into an outright fraud like Madoff. However, I think there are lessons to be learned even for the average investor. First, Madoff's investment funds reported to deliver returns of 2 percent every month. In good markets and in bad, in both low and high interest rate environments, the annualized returns amounted to 24 percent every year. Nobody—I repeat, nobody—can deliver such consistent returns over extended periods of time. There will always be some sort of fluctuation. When there wasn't, it should have been a clue that things weren't as they appeared.

Let's think about those returns: 10 percent to 12 percent each year, with very few losses and hardly any large gains. Unlike Jack's magic beans that actually grew the beanstalk, this fairy tale was too good to be true. If an adviser's promised returns seem above historical returns offered by other advisers, and are always the same each year, it's probably not because you were "lucky" enough to meet him. It's because something just isn't right.

A red flag for Madoff's investors was that the money they gave him to invest was custodied (that is, held by) Madoff's firm. The fact that he had custody also gave him access to their money, which allowed Madoff the ability to surreptitiously remove money from the investors' accounts. When I started The Mutual Fund Store, I also set up a relationship with Schwab Institutional (the division of Charles Schwab & Co. that deals with independent investment advisers) as a firewall between us and our clients' money. As the client's adviser, we have the ability to place trades in the client's account, but we can't take any money out.

Another suspicious fact was that Madoff's auditor was not from a big firm (we use Ernst & Young at The Mutual Fund Store), but rather was a one-man operation in some small New York town. Clients of an investment adviser are not entitled to look at the firm's books; as a privately held company, profits are proprietary. However, I would never have any issue providing a client a letter from our auditors stating that the company is solvent and that they found everything to be in good order. If a firm managing billions of dollars had a rinky-dink auditor, I would be alarmed.

Lastly, and perhaps most importantly, none of the investors really understood what Madoff's investment strategy was. When asked, he reportedly gave vague, convoluted answers using lots of fancy financial terms. His victims were apparently willing to take it on faith (and the recommendations of their friends) that he actually had a strategy. As I have discussed, never invest in something you don't understand.

I'm not saying that you have to understand the inner workings of the strategy—that's why you hire an adviser in the first place. But you do need to know the basic concepts. If I was diagnosed with a disease, I wouldn't need to know the physiology of how a particular treatment works, but I would want to know the general concepts. If a treatment seemed odd to me, I would likely get a second opinion. And, if I ran into a doctor selling a magic snake oil that promised a fast cure with no side effects, I would run away.

I understand the allure of a man like Madoff. He was charming and played to the greedy emotional side of unknowing investors. Although one of the signs described above might not have been enough to ward off potential investors, the combination of all of them should have been a flashing red light.

Understand Your Investments

For the past few decades, major financial services companies in the United States have deliberately tried to make investing seem more complicated than it really is. If a product has a prospectus that's one hundred pages long—or so big that the company gives you a CD to bring home—it's very likely that you will not read the entire thing. And if you do read the entire prospectus, you'll find that it is littered with financial jargon and disclosures, so you may not understand it. Financial companies tend to make investing seem more difficult than it really is because they want you to rely on them and pay for their advice.

The financial services industry has also become very savvy at selling the "new and improved." Why do you think they keep coming out with new exchange-traded funds (ETFs)? It's new—it's extreme—and the marketers try to make you believe you have to be in it. Their strategy has certainly worked: more ETFs were launched in 2007 than in the entire preceding decade. In reality, ETFs are simply index funds that trade like stocks.

Some newfangled financial products can turn out to be very dangerous. Take auction rate preferred securities. These securities were sold by brokers as a money market fund alternative that was supposed to be safe and offer quick access to your cash. They worked like this: closed-end municipal bond funds would sell a preferred stock. At auctions that were supposed to be held each Friday, the muni bond fund would borrow at low short-term interest rates and would buy higher-yielding long-term muni bonds. As a result, these auction rate securities offered a little more yield than a money market fund, and they also enjoyed tax-free status because they were a type of municipal bond.

The first thirteen years that auction rate securities were offered, they worked fine. In 2008, the credit crisis threw them into trouble. The auctions failed, meaning that there was no one to buy the securities. That meant that no one could withdraw any of their money from them, and their value fell. For some investors, it took four or five months to get their money back. One investor told me he had $80,000 tied up in auction rate securities. Another person said he was trying to buy a house and couldn't get the money out of his account in time to close the deal. Investors couldn't have envisioned a scenario in which their money would be frozen in these accounts, because their brokers had pitched them as safe, liquid assets.

The point is, these investors were just trying to get a little more yield to boost returns. But they bought something they didn't understand. It was a complicated product to begin with; then conditions in the market turned against it, and the system failed.

Another example is the collateralized debt obligations (CDOs) that we heard so much about in the 2008 credit crunch. CDOs—essentially portfolios of subprime mortgages—were sold to banks and other institutional investors when the real estate market was booming. When the subprime mortgage market cratered, banks and other companies were left with assets that were worth much less than what they had paid—or became virtually worthless.

Who needed a CDO? Nobody. Who needs a leveraged "30-to-1" energy fund? Nobody. But financial services companies keep creating new products that are hard to understand. For some reason, the more complicated it is, the more people want it.

I have a "new and improved" theory. When you walk down the grocery aisle, you'll see the "new and improved" laundry detergent that promises to make your clothes brighter or "new and improved" toothpaste that claims to whiten your teeth. Now there's "Extreme Doritos." And "Vitamin Water"! How about 100 SPF sunscreen? Do we really need these things? My point is, new and improved may be fine for selling toothpaste, but there's something to be said for the tried and true products that perform as they should.

In the investment world, I can accomplish anything I need to accomplish with mutual funds. For any asset class and diversification, I can buy a mutual fund. If I want to be conservative, for example, I can invest in a fund that invests in Treasury bonds.

Sure, talking about asset allocation and mutual funds doesn't sound exciting. There's really no cool factor here. And those uncool mutual funds, as a whole, won't blow up the way CDOs have.

There are a couple of other investments that readers often buy without properly understanding how they work. These include variable life insurance and annuities. I'm going to explain why you should avoid them.

The Costly Difference between Term and Variable Life Insurance

Life insurance has a simple purpose. It is designed to replace the income of somebody who is no longer with us. I have a wife and three kids. I want to know that if I die tomorrow my wife and children can still live in the same home that we live in now, they can buy groceries and everything else they need, my kids will go to college—in short, my family will enjoy the same lifestyle that they are leading now.

It is a simple mathematical formula to figure out how much life insurance you need to be able to recreate the income that you have. The best way to achieve that is through term life insurance. If I die while I'm paying my premiums, the company pays my family money. If I don't die while I'm paying my premiums, the company gets to keep all the premiums that I've paid it. There's no investment aspect to it; there's no saving for retirement through it. My family's income stream is protected. There's money to pay for the estate taxes on my business. That's it.

However, there are a lot of people out there who will sell whole life insurance plans such as variable life insurance as investment vehicles. They are, almost without exception, a bad deal. An insurance salesperson will sell it to you by saying, "You can put money into this thing, and when you die we will give your family the money. While you're alive, though, this money will go into mutual funds and it will be invested and then it will grow. You will have value there, whereas term insurance has no value if it is not used."

Here are the facts. When you buy variable life insurance, there are several components to the premium. Say that you pay $100 a month for a variable life insurance policy. Perhaps $75 of it actually goes to pay for the life insurance, of which only $15 gets invested, and the balance covers the insurance company's profits.

Term life insurance works differently. Insurance companies offer thirty-year term policies. You buy the insurance today and they guarantee you that premium rate for the next thirty years. For many people, that's an adequate term. Once your kids are grown and once your house is paid for, the need for replacement income diminishes.

Compare costs: with variable life insurance, out of your $100 monthly premium you get the benefit of just $75, and an investment potential for only $15 of that. A comparable term policy, one that pays the same death benefit, may cost only $50 a month.

The insurance company, of course, prefers that you pay the higher premium and fees. However, with the variable life policy you get to invest only $15 of your $100 premium payment each month. If you buy a term policy for $50 a month, then you'll have the other $50 a month to invest—more than three times what you would be investing with the variable life policy!

Don't Fall for Annuities

Another insurance product to avoid is annuities. The variable annuity is basically a family of mutual funds issued through insurance companies instead of directly by the mutual fund company. Nobody wants an annuity. People are *sold* annuities. Nobody wakes up in the morning and says, "I think I'll buy an annuity today." Instead, some guy comes along and says, "What you need is an annuity!"

In the sales pitch, an insurance agent will tell you that the value of an annuity grows tax deferred. If you put $100,000 into it today and over the next ten years it grows to $200,000, that growth is tax deferred: there are no taxes on that $100,000 of growth until you start withdrawing. This may appeal to someone earning a large salary who is not eligible to benefit from a Roth IRA or a tax-deductible IRA.

Agents and brokers tout annuities as a can't-lose proposition: investments in mutual funds wrapped with an insurance feature. An insurer could guarantee a return of 3 percent on a mutual fund within an annuity—even in periods when the stock market is down. So if the market rises, clients benefit. And if the market falls, they won't lose any money, or may even get at least a 3-percent return. That sounds tempting to most investors, especially when stocks have fallen as precipitously as they have in 2008. They want the upside but no downside.

The problem is, when an insurance company makes guarantees like that, it needs to have the capital to back it up. In 2008, the credit crisis drove the huge insurance company American International Group to seek the government's help to prevent its complete failure. If the market doesn't get better, more insurance companies could go out of business. What will happen to their guarantees? Frankly, no one knows.

Still, the heavy marketing of annuities is likely to continue, especially when insurance companies think they can win more customers who are scared of losing money in the stock market. When you see or hear a pitch for an annuity, try to see through the gimmicks. The devil is in the details. These annuities are sold through a prospectus that is typically hundreds of pages thick. My guess is most investors don't ever read a prospectus. Some do, but most take the word of the person who sold it to them. In almost every situation it's not quite as good as it seems. I am one of the few people in America who will read a prospectus. After carefully reviewing the literature accompanying annuities, you have to wonder why anyone would buy them.

One of the main reasons not to buy annuities is that you'll get hit with a higher tax rate if you withdraw money from them. Again, in an annuity, like a 401(k) or an IRA, the growth is tax deferred. But when you take the money out it is taxed at ordinary income rates, which currently run as high as 35 percent at the federal level and may go higher in the future. Compare that with mutual funds, for which the large majority of earnings are taxed at the current long-term capital gains rate of 15 percent.

Let's assume that you invest $100,000 in a mutual fund and that money increases in value over the next several years to $200,000 and then you take the money out. The $100,000 profit is taxed at 15 percent and you are left with a net $185,000.

Consider the same scenario of $100,000 growing to $200,000—except you've invested it in *an annuity*. The $100,000 gain is taxed at 35 percent and you are left with $165,000 after taxes. You've essentially given up what is likely the lowest tax rate that somebody could pay, opting instead for an investment taxed at a very high tax rate.

Proponents of annuities point to the tax-deferred benefit. Well, with all the extra fees associated with annuities, I doubt an annuity's tax-deferral advantage would ever catch up to the benefit of the lower tax rate on ordinary mutual funds. Here's the big irony: roughly 70 percent of annuities sold are put into IRA accounts, which are tax deferred anyway.

There are a few other bad features that you'll encounter in annuities:

Teaser rates. An annuity may pay 8 or 9 percent for the first year. After that it goes to "market rate," which is arbitrarily set by the insurance company. They'll say, "We'll pay the market rate, *which will never be lower than* the guaranteed rate." The guaranteed rate typically is 3 percent.

That reminds me of a promo at one of my favorite barbecue restaurants. They'll give you $5 off if you get a randomly printed red star on your receipt. In my twenty years of eating at this restaurant every Sunday, I've scored that red star one darn time. And that's about how often an insurance company will pay above its guaranteed rate on annuities. So in the end, you buy a product that returns 9 percent for one year but 3 percent for fourteen years.

You might as well stuff your money under the mattress. The insurance companies know that they will have to pay out guarantees to about as many people as win the Powerball lottery.

Surrender periods. Seven years is a common surrender period, which means a client who withdraws money from that annuity before seven years will pay a penalty of as much as 10 percent. I have seen annuities with surrender periods that last fifteen years.

Advisers know how to get around this problem. When a client questions the surrender period, the adviser counters: "But you're a long-term investor, aren't you? This won't ever affect you." Well, let's say your car breaks down, or you need a lawyer for a wayward son. Maybe you decide you and your spouse want to splurge on a second honeymoon. Whatever. You need or want the money, so you try to dip into that annuity or even sell it.

"OK," says the adviser, "but there's a $750 penalty." Ouch. So you decide to keep this bad investment. You still need money, so you sell one of your good investments, something more liquid. That's a double whammy!

I've said it many times, but it bears repeating here: invest only in products in which your eventual decision to hold or sell can be based strictly on the underlying merits of the investment—not on any penalty that may be attached to it.

Cost. Annuities are sold at a very high commission—at least 5 percent, but typically 7 to 10 percent, which is steeper than for just about any other product a commission-based broker sells. Now you see why annuities are so beloved in the industry, and why they are urged onto investors so fervently.

To support those high commissions, insurance companies slap on another layer of annual fees, usually 1.5 to 3.5 percent. That's on top of the management fees already charged by the mutual fund companies. Think of it this way: say you invest in a mutual fund on your own, and invest in that same mutual fund within an annuity. Because of its higher fees, the annuity fund automatically returns 1.5 to 3 percent less. What's more, the broker gets paid up front, so if the investment does well or poorly, it matters little to him financially. He's already taken his cut.

Now think about that surrender period. In six or seven years the broker calls and says, "Hey, remember that annuity you bought? The surrender period is up, and there's a new, better annuity product. Let's move your money into that one."

If you follow his advice, the broker generates another commission. Is he recommending that change because it's better for you or because he wants to boost his income?

You may be thinking, "Adam, you're just being a skeptic." Am I? Waddell & Reed was nailed with more than $15 million in fines and restitution back in 2005 for the sort of activity I've just described. According to the Financial Industry Regulatory Authority (FINRA), they developed an aggressive marketing strategy that encouraged their sales force to increase commissions by pushing clients into new annuities.

I must confess that I used to sell annuities years ago, before I started The Mutual Fund Store. Back then I didn't realize how wrong they were for clients. I was young and naive, and the company I worked for taught me how to sell them, and I made really high commissions.

If annuities are ultimately such a poor investment, you may wonder, why hasn't there been more of an outcry about their downside? Why do annuity sales continue to swell—now surpassing $2 *trillion* in assets? I shake my head at that, too. The reality, unfortunately, is the insurance industry lobby is very strong, and a lot of people make very good money selling annuities. They do an amazing job of protecting that income stream.

I've been on my anti-annuity crusade for so long that some people may wonder whether I have an ax to grind. Perhaps, they think, the insurance industry did me wrong. Not at all. It's just that I consider myself a champion for the average investor—an investor who must make the right choices in the face of an industry that is very large, powerful, and adept at marketing. I even concede that if you feel you must buy an annuity, at least buy one that's inexpensive, with the lowest fees and commission, not one of the ones with the biggest gimmicks.

Clearly, though, a person would sign up for an annuity only if he or she failed to understand the specific characteristics of the investment and had not evaluated purchasing term life insurance along with investing the difference in a diversified portfolio of mutual funds. This illustrates Commandment #7: you should never commit your money to an investment proposition that you do not fully understand. You must make sure that you have an investment adviser who is on your side, willing and capable to fully explain the various investments open to you and not out to steer your money into an investment vehicle that is not in your best interest.

Also, try not to get sucked into the get-rich-quick mentality that has pervaded our society. For some reason, we want to have certain things at our fingertips now. We want our food so fast that we order it through a speaker and drive up to a window to pick it up a few minutes later. Then we eat our Happy Meals in the car, instead of enjoying a healthy meal at home. Getting rich or meeting your goals is not going to happen overnight, unless you beat all odds and win the lottery. You must take the time to research and understand an investment before jumping in. And then you must keep an eye on how your investments are doing. That brings us to our next commandment: be proactive about managing your retirement investments.

BE PROACTIVE ABOUT MANAGING YOUR RETIREMENT INVESTMENTS

There are no scholarships for retirement.
You have to make the most of your opportunities
to invest now so you can retire when and where you want.

NOW THAT YOU HAVE ESTABLISHED your goals and have learned which investments to consider and which to avoid, don't forget about your financial plan. You need to be an active participant in your investments—especially your retirement account, because this is the one financial goal that only you can build and nurture. No one is going to hand you a lump sum the day you retire. You can't apply for a scholarship or grant, and you can't get a loan from the government or bank to pay for your retirement. You need to take control of your nest egg.

During your working years, you should automatically contribute a portion of your salary to your employee retirement plan. But that alone is not enough. Many people think: "I'm contributing to my 401(k), so I'm doing my part." If you don't have a 401(k) or 403(b) plan available to you, open a traditional IRA or Roth IRA account.

Think of it like the regular maintenance that's needed for your car and home. I put gas in my car, but every few months the oil has to be changed and the tires need air. I have service done on my heater and air conditioning units every year to make sure they function properly. You also need to service your retirement accounts on a regular basis.

Before we talk more about how to manage your retirement plan, let's make sure you are properly funding your retirement accounts. The trick is figuring out how much money you'll need in your golden years.

Will You Have Enough Money to Retire?

One of the great investment debates of our times focuses on how much money we'll need in retirement. There are a handful of back-of-the-envelope formulas. One suggests you start with your income now, then lop off 20 percent, the reasoning being that you can probably get by on less once you hit retirement. For a working couple who collectively make $100,000 a year now, that translates to $80,000 they'll need each year to live comfortably in retirement.

That stream of cash might come from several sources. Social Security benefits could net them, say, $20,000 a year, leaving them about $60,000 shy. Which gets to the real question of this exercise: how big must their nest egg be to spin off $60,000 a year? Assuming a reasonable

6 percent annual return over time, they'll need about $1 million socked away.

Now, there are a ton of rough assumptions in these calculations, including tax rates, whether you'll dip into your retirement account to pay for a large purchase, and whether you'll cut back on your living expenses in retirement. In fact, we used to tell people they'd need just 60 or 70 percent of their income at retirement. But some folks envision themselves spending *more* during retirement, what with all those vacations and dinners with friends. And now we're living longer and are more active in our twilight years. Another thing to consider is that you may face higher medical expenses when you're older.

This means we'll need to grow larger nest eggs. It's sort of like retirees years ago had to pack enough food for a weekend campout, whereas now they've got to plan for an expedition up Mt. Everest. There's a good online calculator at Mutualfundstore.com where you can plug in lots of different financial scenarios.

Whatever magical number you have in mind for your retirement account, know this: Most people who build significant wealth don't inherit it, win the lottery, or sell a business. They get rich by saving small amounts of money on a recurring basis over an extended amount of time. In other words, they do the routine stuff over and over, such as contributing a little bit to their 401(k) each paycheck, year after year.

I'm not talking *filthy* rich, mind you. This approach likely won't get you a mansion in Beverly Hills and a collection of Ferraris. But it can get you to that sweet spot of good financial planning—critical mass. It's where your nest egg has grown large enough that you're making as much money from your investments as you do from working full time. That's nirvana, the goal. At this point you can live as comfortably *not working* as you did when you were going full-bore in your career.

How to Save and Invest for Retirement

Since we're talking numbers and formulas, you may wonder just how much of your paycheck you should put into your 401(k). As soon as you start working, contribute at least enough to gain your employer's full match. Some folks say their company match is only 3 percent of their pay, so that's all they're putting in. That's not enough. Shoot for at least 6 or 7 percent. If you can swing it, contribute even more. When you get a raise, for instance, try to sock half of it away for retirement. Ideally, if you start young and eventually are able to send 10 percent of your paycheck to your retirement account, you should be in great shape.

Another way to get there is by contributing small chunks of cash every month. For example, set aside $50 from each paycheck—that's $100 a month, or $1,200 a year—and channel it into a retirement account. Do it for forty years at an 8-percent return and you wind up with about $335,000 before taxes. (This doesn't include any matching contributions from your employer.) What's truly amazing is that your own contributions make up just 14 percent of that bundle. The rest, about $287,000, comes from interest and compounding.

Consider a worker who starts investing in her employer's 401(k) at age twenty-five. She starts at a decent wage—let's say $40,000 a year. She gets a 3.5-percent raise each year, barely beating the average inflation rate. No way this woman will ever be a millionaire, right? Check this out: She contributes a modest 6 percent of her paycheck to the 401(k), with her employer providing a match of 50 cents for each dollar she puts in up to 6 percent of her income. For forty years her account grows at a reasonable 8 percent a year. By the time she retires, her account has reached—get this—almost $1.4 million! And that's all from diverting a drop in the bucket from her paycheck. That's how most of the millionaires next door are made.

But you have to start now. On my radio program, one of the most common questions is from young workers. They convince themselves that once they've socked away $10,000 in their bank account, that's when they'll start investing for the long term. The problem, I tell them, is that while the money is sitting in their checking account it's so tempting to splurge on a new outfit, maybe a night at the ball game, or a couple of extra Christmas gifts.

The solution: don't let that money get anywhere near a checking account! Set up an automatic withdrawal so it goes straight to a retirement plan. The reason the government moved to automatic income-tax withholding from paychecks after World War II is the same reason you should automatically withhold for your retirement: it's a forced, painless withdrawal on a regular basis. Out of sight, out of mind.

The wonderful thing about a 401(k) is that the money you save each month, plus the money that you would otherwise pay in taxes, can grow. If you take $3,000 of earnings in a year and put it into your 401(k) account, that sum immediately starts growing and compounding for you. If you receive the same $3,000 as pay, you are going to give up roughly $1,000—or one-third—in taxes. If you invest the remaining $2,000, it has to grow 50 percent to equal the sum you could have parked—pretax—in your 401(k) account.

On top of that, as I've mentioned, most employers will match a portion of the funds you place into a 401(k). A company may match 50 percent of your investment up to, say, 5 percent of your income. So if you earn, say, $1,000 a week and earmark $50 of it for a traditional 401(k), that $50 will not be subject to federal income tax, and it will trigger an additional 401(k) contribution by your employer of $25—that's $25 you will not get from your employer if you are *not* in the 401(k)!

Here's one important note about 401(k)s. The worker we just described is actually far from typical, of course, because her story assumes she'll work for the same employer from age twenty-five to sixty-five. Most of us will change jobs a number of times; it's very rare for anyone to stay at one company for his or her entire career. When we move from employer to employer, we often can elect to either keep our 401(k) in place with our past employer, move it into a new 401(k) with our new employer or to a traditional IRA account, or simply cash out our investment and receive a check for the sum we have managed to save. I recommend having the money rolled over to a self-directed IRA, because you then have many more investment options available to you. Or you could have the money rolled over to your new employer's 401(k). Both options enable you to proceed with bulking up your savings and sticking to your investment plan. However, 80 percent of people changing jobs elect to take a lump-sum payment for the retirement money they have painstakingly built up over the years. This has several negative effects. It triggers a penalty charge and taxes on the proceeds they receive. Perhaps more important, it is a retreat in their effort to stay on plan to achieve their financial ambitions.

Pay Attention to Your Retirement Accounts

It's not enough to simply sock away money—you also need to monitor your investments. The trouble is, many people treat their 401(k)s and other retirement accounts like the roof over their home—it's there, and that's fine. Far too many employees pick their investment options and then let 'em ride year after year. In fact, just one in six 401(k) participants *ever* changes his investment lineup.

For most people, the 401(k) is their largest retirement asset. The better the account performs during its early accumulative stage, the more income the employee will have in the end. Mutual funds and other options in a 401(k) and other retirement accounts are not a "buy and forget" investment. I don't mean you should noodle with your investment selections every day, but you should evaluate them at least a couple of times a year.

During your investing life span, the volatility of your returns will typically zigzag wildly during the early years, because your portfolio will be invested more aggressively—but that gives you the opportunity for higher average returns. Note that at any given time your actual return can be well below the average. As you approach retirement, you should scale back the risk to reduce volatility. But this also causes the average return to level off.

This isn't a horse race, where the jockeys riding the thoroughbreds cut loose and go for broke when they hit the home stretch. For them, there's no sense in holding back as they speed to the finish line. However, with investing, that's the time when you need to be the most careful. Rein it in. It's true that you need some growth components in your portfolio, but approaching retirement is not the time to take unnecessary risks and make mistakes. There's no time to recover the losses from a bad investment when you're only a couple of years from retirement.

There's still an opportunity for some growth in the home stretch, but this is accomplished with bond funds, balanced funds, and other conservative investments that reduce risk. So don't try to make one more big killing in the market as you're approaching retirement. If you need money to be there, pull in the reins just a bit.

Although there's a need to lower your investment risk as you approach retirement, that doesn't mean you should avoid risk entirely. That's partly because you still want to capture some of the growth opportunities in the market. You'll also need to offset inflation.

The amount of money you spend each year in retirement is likely to go up simply due to the rate of inflation. This makes it necessary to draw more money out each year than you did the year before. An investment portfolio that may have seemed sufficient to accommodate your lifestyle at age sixty-five may need to grow to accommodate that same lifestyle at seventy-five, eighty-five, ninety-five, and beyond. How much growth depends on the size of your portfolio, how much you expect to spend each year, your rate of return, the rate of inflation, and possibly how much you intend to leave in your estate.

Yes, it's important to have a stable value or fixed-income component to your portfolio so it's not significantly affected by market declines. But if you don't give yourself an opportunity for growth, you could deplete your funds too quickly. That could force you to make some tough choices.

There are a few other roadblocks and blunders that you will encounter along the road to retirement. But don't worry. There are ways to solve the problems, and help is easy to find.

Avoid Common Retirement Investment Mistakes

The most common problem that I come across is people will contribute to their retirement plan at work, but they don't know how to pick the right funds. In fact, this is the most frequent question that I get asked on my radio show. When you get a new job, your human resources representative will hand you a folder with your W4 tax form, a description of health benefits, and a list of funds offered in the company's 401(k). Before you sign up for the 401(k), you might ask a friend or your parents, or maybe your new colleague sitting in the next cube, about which funds they like. Or maybe you'll just guess. Eeny meeny miney mo, pick some funds and hope they grow!

By now you probably know what I'm going to say. Don't guess and randomly pick the funds for your 401(k). Your dad and the guy sitting in the next cube have different needs and risk profiles that probably don't apply to you. Picking the funds in your 401(k) is just too important to fool around with. This is your retirement money. The ultimate outcome of your retirement plan at work depends on how those funds perform.

It surprises me that when people are shopping for a new car, they will drive all over town going to different car dealerships to save a few hundred dollars. But they won't spend any time at all to examine the funds in their retirement accounts!

That's why I started Smart401k.com—a service that helps employees choose the right funds in their retirement plan. Here's how it works: first you answer ten questions about yourself, and then a live investment advisor will recommend the funds that best suit you and the dollar amount that you should put in each one. The cost is $200 a year. Companies have started to buy this service for their employees to help them make the best choices.

You certainly don't have to use a service like this. But don't throw a dart and hope you hit a bull's-eye. Evaluate the offerings in your 401(k) and pick the ones that meet your chosen asset allocation (discussed in chapter 4).

On my radio show I've also heard many callers complain that their 401(k) investment choices are few or poor quality. Companies limit the number of investment vehicles open to us in our 401(k)s for an obvious reason: the simplification of our choices is the main way our employer can limit the cost of offering employees a 401(k) option. Instead of contributing to their 401(k), employees wonder whether they should take the money as regular salary and invest it in better funds on their own and house them in an IRA.

The answer to this question is you should always put your money in the 401(k). The compounding and tax benefits you get from the 401(k) make the poor funds good and good funds great. If the employer matches your contribution, then it is a no-brainer. You can ask your human resources representative about getting better fund options.

I've also seen 401(k)s bulging with the investor's own company stock. Now, I know you want to show pride and confidence in your employer, but there are smarter ways than stuffing your retirement plan with the company's stock. This is the company that's putting food on your table and keeping a roof over your head. Why would you also risk your retirement on the same company? (And don't tell me your top executives won't screw up. The folks at WorldCom and Enron believed the same thing.)

Think about a car. It has dual diagonal brakes, one from the front-left wheel to the right-rear wheel, the other from the right-front wheel to the left-rear wheel. If one line is severed, you'll still be able to stop, but not as fast. Loading up on company stock in your 401(k) is like driving with only one brake line. It's flat-out dangerous.

By avoiding company stock in your 401(k), you're not saying your employer isn't trustworthy or honorable. You just need a safety net. What if you're offered company stock at a discount? Go ahead and buy if you want, but don't let your company stock account for more than 10 percent of your entire portfolio.

Many employers will allow participants to borrow money from their 401(k) accounts. The allure of a loan sounds attractive: you'll be borrowing the money from yourself and all of the interest goes right back into your 401(k).

I believe that taking a loan from your 401(k) should only be used in a last, final, "I have no other possible options" situation. Common sense will tell you that you shouldn't use a retirement plan loan to pay for new clothes, a vacation, or that flat-screen TV. It may be more tempting, however, to use one to pay off credit cards, a student loan, or some other monthly expense that's putting some strain on your budget. The problem is that like many things in life, for most people it's easier to take the money out than to put it back in.

That 401(k) loan will have to be paid back, out of monthly payroll deductions. And, if for any reason you separate employment (get laid off or even quit to take a better job) the loan will have to be paid back immediately in full. If you don't, you will be required to pay state and federal income taxes on the outstanding loan balance, as well as a 10 percent penalty if you are under age 59½. While most people take these loans with the best of intentions, it's just too easy to rack up new credit card balances once the monthly burden is lifted. Next thing you know, they end up with a new set of debt *and* the 401(k) loan.

I see plenty of other 401(k) mistakes. Afraid to lose any money, some people channel all their contributions into money market accounts. Sure, they have no market risk, but they face inflation risk. If the money market pays 4.5 percent but inflation is at 3 percent, then they're making only 1.5 percent a year.

The other common mistakes that you can make with your investments (which we talked about in chapter 1) also apply to your retirement accounts. These include being too passive about your investments, ignoring a bad investment and holding it too long, and being too emotional about your decisions.

These days, there's so much financial information at your fingertips. You certainly don't want to be obsessively checking your 401(k) every day if your company allows you to view your account online. Instead, review your holdings twice a year, and stick to your plan. Make sure the funds you're invested in are doing what they are supposed to do, and make changes when necessary. In the next chapter, I'll explain how to stick to your plan to keep you on the road to financial success.

STICK TO YOUR PLAN

If you react emotionally to the markets,
you are going to buy and sell the wrong things at the wrong time.

ONE OF THE SECRETS to successful investing is discipline. You have put a lot of thought and effort into building your financial plan and choosing the right mutual funds. Now all you have to do is stick to your plan. It sounds simple enough, but it's not easy for everyone. The problem is, if you stray from your plan and suddenly switch gears, your portfolio will probably suffer and you'll have trouble meeting your goals.

Staying focused on your plan can be quite challenging, especially with the explosion of financial data everywhere and the various opinions of so many market experts appearing in magazines and websites and on TV. Some experts are worth listening to (especially me!), but you shouldn't make investing decisions based on what an expert says in one interview, because this may not describe the whole picture. And tomorrow the expert could be singing a completely different tune.

When the credit crisis threw the markets into a tailspin in autumn 2008, the story of the government's bailout of financial firms and Lehman Brothers' bankruptcy moved from the financial press to the mainstream media. *Good Morning America, The View,* and even *Oprah* talked about the tighter lending conditions, home foreclosures, and the falling stock market, and they scared the heck out of people. With news reports of steep job losses and companies struggling and even going bankrupt, it's understandable that people were nervous during this recession. I heard some people say they stopped contributing to their 401(k) because they were so worried. But making drastic changes to your plan during bad times is not a good idea.

Sure, it's very difficult to stick with your plan when you see stocks going down and all you hear is doom and gloom. Although it's convenient to have access to your 401(k) and other investment accounts online, try not to check them every day. The more you look at your account, the more volatile it will seem—and the more you'll be tempted to make changes.

If you have planned correctly and considered your risk tolerance, your investment psyche should not suffer too much damage in bad times, because you've already taken into account that stocks don't go up all of the time. As you stay focused and continue putting money into your retirement accounts and other investments, your dollar cost averaging and well-planned investing strategy will pay off in the long run.

Of course, if you have a significant change in your circumstances—say, you get laid off, or someone in your immediate family develops a serious illness—that's when you can modify your plan. But don't make big changes just because the market is behaving badly for a few months or years.

Learn How to Sit Still

Back in kindergarten, we were taught to raise our hands before speaking. That's tough on a five-year-old, especially for a kid like me who had a lot to say. I had to learn the system: raise your hand and get called on before speaking.

That urge to spontaneously act continues to burn fiercely in many of us. Markets turn volatile and people itch to do *something*. We can't just sit on our hands. Through the mid- and late 1990s, there was a rush to put all investments in stocks. Then the market buckled, and folks scrambled to move all their money to bonds.

Day-to-day market gyrations have long been a fact of life. The Dow may drop 1,000 points today. That's the little picture. The big picture is this: sometimes the market goes down before going up. That's the price we pay for better returns. Rather than trying to time that swing, you need to just . . . sit on your hands.

There's another problem when you sell during a declining market. Now you must decide *when to jump back in*. That's hard. Let's say you sell near the bottom of a cycle—which many people do. Now you're scared to put your skin back in the game. If the market rises, it's higher than when you sold. Now you have to pay a higher price to get back the same things you used to own. And if it drops further? "Well, it will probably continue to decline," you think. Who knows how much of the initial bounce you'll miss before you bite the bullet and jump back in?

At this rate you'll never make money! That's why we have this beautiful thing called asset allocation, which really is nothing more than finding a way to spread your money sensibly among different types of investments. And that, friends, gives you diversification: a pillar of sound investing.

Look, the market will go through cycles—everyone loves tech stocks, then we hate 'em. Same goes for international stocks and Treasury bonds. I'm never going to be smart enough or lucky enough to say today is the day we should put all your money into tech stocks, then move your money into Treasury bonds tomorrow. But if you have asset allocation— the right mix of exposure to different stocks and bonds, to small cap and large cap, to domestic and growth stocks, to international stocks and value stocks—you can weather just about any market environment.

Sure, in a down market the stock segment of your portfolio will decline. But other types of investments will serve as ballast to counterbalance your losses. Over many months and years, if you can earn more when markets rise and lose less when they fall, then your average returns over the long haul will be impressive.

Do Not Let Your Emotions Rule

As time goes by, some investors let their emotions steer them away from their plan. For example, an investor determines that to achieve a goal she needs to save and invest $1,000 a month. Every month, $1,000 gets invested into her 401(k) retirement account or mutual funds. Then along comes a year like 2008 and the market goes down. Way down. The investor tells herself, "I put $12,000 into this thing in 2008 and now it's worth $10,000. I can live with that." A few weeks later, her $12,000 investment is worth $9,000. Now the investor tells herself, "I'm not doing this anymore. I'm not going to pour more money into a losing proposition." So she liquidates her holdings just before the market registers a significant rebound.

Some people have horrible timing. They will buy when stock valuations are at an all-time high and sell when stocks probe record lows. These people let emotions rule. I have some clients who put together a plan and are doing great, but they can't just sit back and watch it grow. They have to do something. They will call me and say: "We own the XYZ fund and it made 24 percent last year in a market that was up 20 percent. But we have found a fund that was up 29 percent, so let's move our money into this new fund."

I will point out that the fund they currently hold has outperformed the market for several consecutive years—and they should stay with it. They don't care. Some people are tinkerers. Many times you hurt yourself by doing that—because you abandon your plan!

Do Not Tinker with Your Investments

If you're uneasy with the level of volatility in your investments, it just means your allocation wasn't appropriate to begin with. Readjust your asset allocations so that when you hear about a big shift in the day's market—up or down—it doesn't faze you.

We went through the bear market of 2000–2002, and we had another one in 2008. These precipitous market drops can cause people to reevaluate their risk tolerance. That's fine, as long as it's a well-thought-out change based on how comfortable you are with movements in your investments, and you're not letting your emotions take over.

Here's another tip: don't follow the herd. Be your own shepherd. It's dangerous to decide that you have to be in stocks just because they're going up and everyone is piling in. It's just as silly to get out of them when the market is going down and everyone is crying wolf. Try to maintain moderation all around—your investments don't have to be an all-or-nothing proposition.

What ultimately moves the market is fear and greed. One day there is fear of loss, and the next day it turns to fear of missing out on the returns. I've learned that the smartest way to invest is to stick with boring, tried-and-true investments. I do like excitement—I enjoy racing cars, scuba diving, and anything that goes fast—but not when it comes to my serious money. There are many other ways to have fun.

Stay Upbeat and Disciplined

Too often, investors unwittingly throw up barriers to achieving their financial objectives. I'm certainly not a psychiatrist, but from working with clients through the years I've noticed that some folks are flat-out pessimistic about their investments and their lives. Maybe their favorite team won—but won ugly. Or they get front-row seats but grumble that they're too close to see the whole field. Their investments climbed for the quarter but were shy of the benchmark. Surely the market can't continue to rise.

I've witnessed this gloomy nature in some of my clients, and I'm convinced it really does hamper their ability to prosper and enjoy life. Maybe they need to delegate more. Should they wear a Pollyanna smile? No, but I believe in my heart that good things do indeed happen when we stay upbeat and look for the positive in our lives each day. And if you stick to your plan and stay focused, your financial rewards will be great.

Commandment **#10**

LIVE WELL,
FOR YOU CANNOT
TAKE IT WITH YOU!

Save for retirement, but not at the expense of enjoying life now.

I AM AN AVID INVESTOR and try to help people get on the road to financial success. I am also a car aficionado. I own some cool cars, not because it impresses anyone else, but because it makes me happy. I grin from ear to ear whenever I spend time in my cars. If you work hard and are actively saving and investing for your future, you deserve to treat yourself. You should travel to places you've always wanted to explore and do the things that make you happy. Of course, you should not spend money on things you can't afford and mess up your long-term financial plan. But you want to enrich your life.

I try to enjoy life while I'm still young and healthy. I'm in my mid-forties while writing this book, and I know several people who are plus or minus ten years from my age who have gotten cancer. Tragic things have happened to them, and their lives were cut short. Sometimes people will put off a trip to Machu Picchu or a cruise around the Greek Islands that they've dreamed about because they're too busy at work or they worry about the cost. But if people wait too long and don't take those trips or do things that make them happy, their later years may be full of regrets.

In Retirement, Switch from Saving to Spending

I work with a lot of people who are retired. All through their lives they have been told to save. When they reach retirement age, I say to them: "Okay, now you are going to start spending your money." Many of them just can't deal with that. They may point out, "My account is producing $5,000 a month in income and if I spend $5,000 a month then it won't be growing anymore." Well, yes—that's the idea. But the notion is simply foreign to them. You may as well tell them to fly to the moon. Saving has become a habit. Saving has served them well. Many retirees cannot comfortably make the transition into spending their hard-earned savings and investment income.

I explain to them that they can possibly earn 10 percent a year by holding a combination of stocks and bonds. For some clients who are a little more risk-averse, maybe we can earn 8 percent. For a typical sixty-year-old who has had stock market experience and believes he is going to live for an additional twenty to thirty years, a 10-percent return is a possible investment objective. Keep in mind that the stock market can have a very strong performance one year and a deep decline the next.

Of course, everyone's great fear is possibly running out of money. Again, if you are comfortable assuming some risk associated with investments that have the possibility to generate a 10-percent rate of return and you spend 7 percent and reinvest 3 percent, you should be well positioned for a healthy retirement.

Ultimately, of course, our clients' money is their money. I never tell clients how much to regularly withdraw from their accounts. That said, however, there are certain commonsense considerations for retirees. It makes little sense for them to live their lives in such a manner that they die with a zero net worth.

It also is pointless for investors to fully preserve their life savings to transmit to heirs as an inheritance. When you die, whether you leave your children $250,000, $500,000, or $1 million, they should be appreciative, because that is money that *you* worked for—not money *they* worked for. Regardless of what the amount is, it is a bonus for them. On the other hand, if you can do some things in your life before you die that bring you a little more pleasure, I say do it. In all likelihood, your children will be gratified to know your last years were lived—and enjoyed—in grace and comfort.

Giving Feels Good

Giving to charity is one of the most rewarding acts you can do. If you don't want to donate money, donating your time is just as good. Sometimes we get so caught up in our work and daily lives that it's easy to forget that not everyone is as fortunate as we are to have health and wealth. When you give back, not only does it help someone, but you'll also feel like you've done something very worthwhile. You just can't put a price on that.

We have set up The Mutual Fund Store Foundation to make "last chance" grants that are smaller in nature but make a big difference in people's everyday lives. We figure that the philanthropic community is set up to handle big issues like finding a cure for cancer and providing disaster relief. Medicaid will pay for someone in economic need to have an eye exam, but they will not pay for glasses. Our grants help pay for glasses for the working poor. We have another grant that pays for bus passes for unemployed people so they can get where they need to be to apply for jobs. It might be only $20 a month for a bus pass, but we're making it possible for someone who couldn't afford it.

Your time and caring can also make a difference. I want to help and also teach others about how to make a difference in the world. So when I do charity work, I take my kids with me so they learn how important it is to give back. My oldest daughter volunteers at a camp with special needs children. At my office, my staff gets involved and organizes projects for charities throughout the year.

I certainly can't tell you what hobbies you should have, but it is important to remember that people need help. From our foundation, I have read stacks of letters from people whom we've helped. That's money that I can't take with me. It feels so good.

You Can Be a Great Investor, Too

What does it mean to be a "great" investor?

Most people don't become great investors overnight. There are many lessons to be learned, and mistakes will be made along the way. First, it's important to know yourself; that is, to know what your time horizons are, understand how much volatility you are emotionally comfortable with, and just as importantly to recognize what you don't know. There is no shame in admitting that you may need some help when making investment decisions.

To get on the road to financial success, devise a written plan that will take you from your current economic location to where you want to be somewhere in the future. A homebuilder doesn't just start nailing boards together until they look like a house. Rather, he works from a set of blueprints. A great investor does the same with his or her investments.

Another important trait of the great investor is the self-discipline to periodically review your investment plan and investment holdings on a recurring basis, and to do so in a conscientious, rational manner without letting the emotions of current market conditions affect your decisions. Make sure you're comfortable with any swings in the value of your portfolio—if you're not sleeping well at night, change your asset allocation.

The great investor knows that great wealth is accumulated by investing small amounts of money on a regular basis over long periods of time. As much as we would all like to win the lottery, it's probably not going to happen. And, it's not enough to just participate in a 401(k) or other retirement plan; you must actively monitor and groom your holdings.

Every year the consumer electronics firms bring us cooler new gadgets, food companies make new flavors and snacks, and clothing designers create new fashion looks. While new and improved is exciting when it comes to consumer products, the great investor knows that the improved odds that come with a proven, tried-and-true investment strategy beat the novelty of the "newest" thing.

There are a lot of well-known financial firms who want investment management to seem very complicated. After all, how is a "normal" person supposed to understand stochastic analysis, collateralized debt obligations, or senior subordinated preferred securities? Many investment salespeople will show you a slick brochure and describe what seems to be an almost magical opportunity. The great investor knows that the devil is in the details. A giant prospectus full of small type is theoretically designed to protect the investor; in reality it's also a great place to hide the intricacies of the investment that will only become an issue when you try to get out of it someday in the future.

The great investor knows that it doesn't have to be complicated. The relatively simple strategy of having a diversified portfolio of no-load mutual funds is easy enough for just about anyone to understand. Each person can find a group of no-load funds to fit into their asset allocation that have been top performers for many years and are run by seasoned and successful managers.

Part of being a great investor is being a great person. For every person who reads this book and hopefully provides himself with a viable financial future, there is also someone out there who, either as a victim of circumstances or as a victim of his own poor decisions, needs some help. I can't tell you who or how to help, but I can assure you that it feels darn good.

A great investor doesn't keep his knowledge to himself. A baby doesn't spring from the womb with an instant knowledge of sound investing principles. Our society is plagued by people who are easily swayed by the "I want it now" attitude that has become so pervasive. So, what to do? Share what you've learned with your children, grandchildren, coworkers, or neighbors. Let them know about the mistakes you've made as well as the successes.

Following my ten investment commandments can help you become a great investor. Use this book as a guide to get you on the road to financial success, so that you are living well—whether in retirement or before—and enjoying your life. If I can do it, so can you.

ACKNOWLEDGMENTS

I have the great fortune of working every day alongside talented, hard-working people at The Mutual Fund Store. Thank you all for your time, commitment, and camaraderie. With you, we have grown from a small, two-employee business to a nationwide company.

Thank you to the clients of The Mutual Fund Store for believing in me, the financial advisers, and the staff members who work hard for you. The trust you place in us is something we do not take lightly. Your stories helped develop my thoughts as I prepared the content for this book, and they bring true meaning to our daily work at The Mutual Fund Store.

Thanks also go to the listeners of *The Mutual Fund Show* who faithfully tune in each and every week. Thank you for your calls, emails, and financial questions, as they, too, have helped form the ideas in this book and give me an opportunity to further educate others about economic issues that affect their personal finances.

I will be forever grateful to Peter Newman, the first person to introduce me to the power of radio. Without Peter's invitation many years ago to participate on his radio show, I would not have found the teaching opportunity that continues in my radio show today.

This book would not be possible without the writers and editors who helped develop my thoughts and ideas into clear content. Thank you to Mike Glynn, Martin Rosenberg, and especially to Karyn McCormack, who made this book what it is today.

Thank you to my publisher, Ten Speed Press, for taking on this project. I would like to acknowledge all the dedicated people there who have made this book a priority in their busy days.

INDEX

ABOUT THE AUTHOR

Adam Bold is the founder and CEO of The Mutual Fund Store, the first nationally branded, independent registered investment advisory organization in the United States. Founded by Bold in 1996 and headquartered in Overland Park, Kansas, The Mutual Fund Store locations are found coast to coast, bringing investment advisory services to thousands of Americans.

Fulfilling his goal of sharing his mutual fund knowledge with the average investor, Bold hosts the only nationally syndicated, call-in radio program devoted to mutual funds, *The Mutual Fund Show*. Heard each week across the country, Bold answers listeners' financial questions and shares market and economic commentary.

Bold received the 2006 Ernst & Young Entrepreneur of the Year award after being named a finalist the previous two years. In 2008, he was nominated from a field of three thousand to the Board of Advisors for the Institute of Business & Finance (IBF), the fourth-oldest provider of financial certifications in the United States.

Under the leadership of Bold, The Mutual Fund Store system was recognized in 2008 by *Financial Advisor* as the eighth-largest Registered Investment Adviser in the United States and number two in growth of assets under management (AUM) among firms managing $1 billion or more. *Wealth Manager's* 2008 rankings placed The Mutual Fund Store number one in the number of client relationships and number thirteen in client AUM among financial advisers not registered as broker/dealers, banks, or trusts.

Bold is a Chartered Mutual Fund Counselor (CMFC), a designation awarded by the College for Financial Planning, and a Certified Fund Specialist (CFS), a certification awarded by the Institute of Business &

Finance. As a recognized expert in his field, he is a frequent contributor to Fox Business, CNBC, *SmartMoney, Bloomberg*, and other financial programs and publications.

In addition to his work in the financial services field, he is an avid supporter of charity. With the belief that philanthropy has the power to effect and achieve positive change, Bold established The Mutual Fund Store Foundation. Through "last chance" grants to working-poor families, the foundation helps them remain self-sufficient.